Sifter Stickers

Jack Azout

Copyright © Jack Azout 2008
All rights reserved.

ISBN: 978-0-578-00217-0

Contents

Introduction	vii
OK, Here Goes	1
PC or Not PC	3
The Magic of Passion	5
Public Funds for Sports	9
The Smell of Internet Access	11
The Headache or the Tumor?	13
Walt, You Can't Be Serious!	17
Cursive?	27
Humanity 1.1	29
Hardwired Honesty	31

What's in a Name	35
Fairness in an Unfair World	37
Fill in the Blanks—NOT	41
Halitosis	43
WWDK	47
The Drive to Contrive	51
Just Scan, Man	55
Hephaestus	59
On the Brink	63
Breakfast of Champions	65
Water and Diamonds	67
No, Virginia	71
Freedom	75
Obtrusive	79
Let the Music Take You	81
We're All in Stockholm	83
Windows on the Mac	87
Cynicism	91
The Light Turns Red	95
Nuggets	97
Immigration	99
Diversity	103

Nuggets II	107
Land of . . .	109
Thank You, God	113
The Hard Way	115
Baseball and the News	117
So Many Pieces	119
Sportsmanship	121
TWREoHID	125
Net Neutrality	127
To Do or Not To Do	133
Communism and Youth	135
TWREoHID II	137
Litmus Test	141
WWDC Keynote	145
The Chasm	147
They Should Pay	151
Stubborn Futility	153
TSA	155
Ringtones	157
Zune	161
Gerstein	165
TWREoHID III	167

Inertia	171
GrandCentral	175
Sports and the Holocaust	179
Official Scorer	183
We Have Lost the War	187
On Faith	191
eBay	195
Ratatouille	199
iPhone	201
TWREoHID IV	203
Shades of the Same Hue	207
Anticipation	211
Transcend Attachments	213
So Much Time	217
The Voice of God	221
The Ethanol Myth	225
Ron Wants Out	229
Life in the Cloud	233
The Obama Dilemma	235

Introduction

WHAT STICKS TO your mind? As we go about our daily lives we are bombarded with information—much more information than we can possibly process. So our brains automatically do the only sensible thing they can: they discard most of the information presented to them, processing only what they feel is useful or important to us. Our brains, though, seem to merrily decide what to throw away and what to keep on their own, without really checking with us first, so much information we would consider highly important, even critical, is allowed to fly right past us while useless data is inexplicably captured and stored away.

Further complicating matters, each one of our brains selects information to be captured based on its own unique criteria. So even if you and I happen to be deluged with identical sets of data, the subset of that data that will wind up in my mind will be completely different from the subset that will wind up in yours! One person's discard is another's keeper, based on reasons unbeknownst to us all.

While considering this selection process, the great Stephen King drew a metaphor between the human mind and a sifter, where most of the information presented is filtered through the holes and lost forever, while some of the information sticks to the sifter. While paying tribute to King, whose work I enjoy immensely, the title of my book attempts to explain its contents: essays about material that at some point found itself stuck to the sifter of my mind.

Sifter Stickers, which started life as a blog (hence the original online publishing date at the end of each essay), consists of 73 essays, generally unrelated to each other. You will find some recurring topics, which loosely correspond to areas of interest to me. Perhaps there is some overlap between what your mind and mine have selected as "keeper" material over the years, and you've had similar thoughts about some of the same topics. Or totally dissimilar thoughts, and opposing points of view. Or perhaps some of my mind's selections were never even considered by your mind, in which case you may find the essays about such topics refreshing, infuriating, or of no interest whatsoever.

Reading *Sifter Stickers* will give you a pretty good idea of who I am and where I stand on many topics, but it makes sense to provide you with some background here for initial context as you begin reading my essays. I was born in Barranquilla, Colombia on November 20th, 1961, and did most of my growing up in Bogota (still in Colombia). I immigrated to the United States as a high school student in 1978, became a U.S. permanent resident in 1985, and was proudly sworn in as a U.S. citizen in 1994. I like to tell native-born Americans that, unlike them, I am a U.S. citizen by conscious choice, not by accident of birth. I am ethnically Jewish, but religiously an atheist. I am a Babson College (Wellesley, MA) business graduate.

I've lived in South Florida since 1983, which makes me pretty much a native, as locally defined, and have made Coral Gables my hometown for the past 13 years. I run Prescient

Solutions, a technology consulting firm (for details, please see www.prescientsolutions.com), as well as Electrical Systems International (and its subsidiary, ESI de Colombia), purveyors of engineering services and industrial electrical equipment (www.electricalsystemsintl.com).

Writing about random topics that come to mind is enjoyable to me, mostly because it seems to somehow put the matter to rest. Addressing the topic in an essay helps it stop banging about in my head, bringing some measure of tranquility and making some much needed space for the next item that may come flying in. I hope you enjoy reading about the stuff that sticks to my sifter as much as I enjoyed writing about it!

San Francisco, June 9, 2008

OK, Here Goes

January 16, 2005

WELL, THE INFRASTRUCTURE is set for my blog. That took all of three minutes . . . obviously that is the easy part. Having something worthwhile to say, and saying it with clarity, eloquence and style—that is a whole other matter.

Why am I starting a blog? Difficult to say. I just got back from a week in San Francisco attending Macworld Expo, and as much as I enjoyed the keynote (yes, attending a Steve Jobs keynote live is one of the very few things in life worth standing in the rain at 44 degrees for an hour!), the exhibit hall, the training, and the networking, the two feature presentations (David Pogue and Wil Wheaton) were probably what most impacted me.

David Pogue is astoundingly talented, and every time I am exposed to his work I am once again amazed at his abilities. He writes a weekly column for the *New York Times*, a daily blog on his Web site, all sorts of books, and who knows what else. He produces videos. He performs on stage at various venues. He attends trade shows and other events. He apparently has a great family life. How is he able to do all of that, and do it all so incredibly well? Obviously the short answer is: it's the talent, stupid! But I think it's more than that. I think he's the kind of person who does things first and asks questions later. I tend to ask all sorts of questions before I do anything, and I would like to once in a while simply do something on an impulse. This blog is almost that. "Almost" because I can't honestly say that I just had an impulse to blog a few minutes ago and here I am. I've actually been thinking about it for a couple of weeks. But tonight (or this morning, actually) is when I finally just did it.

I was moved by Wil Wheaton's Macworld presentation. A difficult early childhood, success as a child actor, lack of success as a young adult actor, despair, and finally fulfillment and happiness through family and finding his true vocation: writing. I don't think my true vocation is writing, although it may be a part of it. But I do enjoy writing. So, as Wil did years ago, I will start a blog and see where it goes, having absolutely no idea what the style or content of this blog will eventually be. But then again, that's the whole idea!

PC or Not PC

January 25, 2005

A S WE ALL know, and as Apple Computer kindly reminds us at the end of every press release, "Apple ignited the personal computer revolution in the 1970s with the Apple II and rein-vented the personal computer in the 1980s with the Macintosh." So, why does everyone (including, astoundingly, Apple Computer!) use the term PC to refer to Windows-based computers? As in "PC or Mac"? This usage gives far too much credit to Microsoft, since the implication is that the only Personal Computer, or PC, is a Windows machine, and everything else (including a Mac) is somehow not a personal computer. This does not compute!

For some unknown and overwhelmingly invalid reason, probably having much to do with the fact that IBM's original personal computer was named the IBM PC, and all Wintel computers are direct descendants of that particular machine, Windows computers are the *only* machines deemed worthy of the PC designation. Linux computers are invariably called "Linux boxes," and who knows what other UNIX-based computers are referred to as. (I must ask some of my more UNIX-y friends that question, but you can bet the house and car that they are not known as PCs!). So Windows—the operating system that is basically a badly executed copy of the Mac, which is the legitimate successor to the Apple II, clearly the first mass-market personal computer—gets the PC designation? No, that will not do!

I say we stop this grave injustice now! My suggestion: let's call Windows computers "Windows PCs." That's it. When referring to a Windows computer, never use "PC" without preceding it with "Windows." If we all do our part, the generic "PC" designation will apply, as it should, to any personal computer, be it a Mac-, Windows-, Linux-, or whatever-comes-in-the-future-based machine. Apple, this goes for you too. Please, no more "PC or Mac" at the end of iPod commercials! How about "Windows or Mac"? Sounds good to me!

Update

Of course, far from heeding my suggestions Apple Inc. (the company formerly known as "Apple Computer, Inc.") has done the opposite! Their "Buy a Mac" series of television commercials stars Justin Long as "Mac" and the inimitable John Hodgman as, you guessed it, PC!

The Magic of Passion

February 2, 2005

I RECENTLY HAD occasion to visit the Apple Store at The Falls (Miami, Florida) and immediately follow that with a visit to the CompUSA store across the street. I had been to both places many times, yet never one right after the other. I was astounded by the difference!

Any Apple Store (and The Falls is my personal favorite) is a textbook example of retailing done right. The store designs are well thought out, and the materials used are top notch. The products are displayed attractively, and the demo equipment always works perfectly. Store management and staff are well trained, friendly, and courteous. And, of course, the products themselves are—yes, Steve—insanely great. But as important as those factors are in making the Apple stores successful, they are not what makes the stores really different. No, what makes them different is how the people at the store feel about the products they sell.

The passion felt by every Apple Store employee toward their products envelops the store's atmosphere like the paint covered the world in the old Sherwin Williams ads. Nobody is "selling" you anything; cool people are telling you about the incredibly cool stuff they have, and hey, you can have it too if you want! Every single Apple Store employee lives and breathes Apple, and would love to tell you all about how truly awesome this stuff is. And it shows.

And so I left this wonderful place where everything is cool and everyone is smiling, and arrived at this other place, CompUSA, with 20 times the space, 20 times the products, 20 times the number of people. But the spirit? On a scale of one to ten, as legendary South Florida radio talk show host Neil Rogers would say, it's minus infinity. Supermarket employees show more passion pointing out the canned tomatoes than CompUSA people do talking about the latest HP desktop or Toshiba notebook.

So I strike up a conversation with the CompUSA guy, mentioning, of course, that I'm a Mac consultant. The usual friendly Mac-versus-Windows PC banter ensues, and the interesting thing is, the pro-Windows PC argument boils down to: "Yes, I know it sucks, but look at all the software for it!." And when the conversation turns to viruses and spyware, which are unfathomably out of control on Windows, the guy's answer is, "Well, if you know what you're doing viruses and spyware are not a problem." Sure, that's great. So, what does that say about 95 percent of Windows users for whom it is a problem? What does that say about the fact that none of the computers on display at CompUSA is actually on the Internet—as opposed to the Apple Store, where they are all online?

There's a difference between "This is really cool. I love it myself, and you'll love it too!" and "This sucks but hey, everyone has it. And may I interest you in an extended warranty?"

There is no substitute for genuine passion. Sadly, passion seems to be in short supply in most places, but if you need to remind yourself that it really does exist, just step into your friendly neighborhood Apple Store.

Update

CompUSA's lack of passion proved to be its undoing, or at least part of it, as the once-mighty retailer crashed and burned spectacularly in 2007. Apple's retail store operation, of course, continues to be wildly successful. The magic of passion indeed!

Public Funds for Sports

February 3, 2005

AS I LISTEN to the debate between the City of Miami and the Florida Marlins regarding how many millions of dollars the city should contribute toward the building of a new ballpark, I can't help but reflect on the absurdity of the whole thing. Think about it. Our elected officials are debating how much of our money should go toward paying for a structure that will enable a local business to increase its revenues. Sort of like if the City of Miami were to pay for an office building in which to house my company.

What is it about sports that makes people do things they would not think of doing under other circumstances? Why does the City of Miami feel the need to contribute $60 million (the number being discussed) to help a private business owner, who, based on the salaries he pays his employees, is not exactly in need of financial aid? Why not help other businesses in the local area? Think of how many iBooks the city could place in the hands of schoolchildren with those $60 million (about 60,000 iBooks, in case you're wondering)!

But then again, sports are the exception to lots of rules. Team owners, of course, treat their franchises as businesses. Professional athletes play for whichever team pays them the most, treating their vocation as a business. But when the public treats sports as it would any other business, by, for example, not attending games played by lousy teams, they are branded as "fair-weather fans" and "bandwagon jumpers." Please tell me of another business where customers are made to feel guilty about refusing to purchase a bad product!

I say let's treat professional sports as any other business, and let them stand on their own feet. If the Marlins want to move to Las Vegas, well, yes, I will miss listening to them on the radio every now and again, but I would much rather let them go than pay tens of millions of dollars so that they stay. Or hey, maybe I should jump on that bandwagon and inform Miami-Dade County that if they do not give me $3,000 for a new Dual 2.5GHz Power Mac G5 to run my business I will relocate my company to Broward County!

The Smell of Internet Access

February 8, 2005

I'VE HEARD THAT smell is the most evocative of the senses, and my experience seems to bear that out. Many times when stepping into an elevator or hallway, the particular odor inside has instantly transported me to a specific place and time in my life, sometimes 10, 15, and even 20-plus years in the past.

A place with a unique, identifiable odor is Starbucks Coffee. For many of us, the ubiquitous coffee house has become an office away from the office, or even home away from home as we meet with clients or associates there, or make it a pit stop between appointments to catch up on email, make a few calls, and yes, grab an occasional cup o' Joe. The experience at Starbucks is unique in that you are in a pleasantly bustling atmosphere surrounded by people, yet none of those people interrupts your workflow, unlike a traditional office or home office. So we happily fork over four bucks for a 50-cent cup of coffee, and admire the business acumen of those who thought up the concept and executed it so flawlessly.

Where am I going with the smell thing and Starbucks? Well, we've all heard of Pavlov's legendary dogs, which were found to consistently salivate at the sound of a bell based on prior associations. Much like those mindlessly responsive canines, I find myself associating the smell of Starbucks with Internet access. I guess since on so many occasions my catching a whiff of rich coffee is immediately followed by being online, whenever I I'm exposed to the smell of coffee now I automatically reach for my PowerBook and yearn to fire up Mail and Firefox. Powerful stuff indeed, these subconscious associations.

Sort of makes you think about those rumors about the Disney people flooding their theme parks with the smell of popcorn, which evokes pleasurable experiences for most people, or theorize about more sinister uses of our smell associations.

In any event, although I'm mostly online in places other than Starbucks, to me the smell of freshly brewed coffee is, unmistakably, the scent of the Internet.

The Headache or the Tumor?

February 15, 2005

A FEW NIGHTS AGO my old friend Ed Kaplan said something quite interesting. (By the way, Eddie K is a local late-night radio talk show host who has graced the South Florida airwaves for as long as I can remember, and since I have been listening to him for at least 20 years, usually while getting ready for bed, I consider him an old friend, even though he, of course, has absolutely no idea who I am. Ah, the magic of radio.)

Eddie was talking about New York Yankee first baseman Jason Giambi's recent press conference, during which he apologized to his team and fans, ostensibly for having used steroids for at least three seasons, as he reportedly told a federal grand jury last December. I say ostensibly because during the news conference Giambi did not utter the word "steroids." When asked what he was apologizing for, exactly, Giambi was bizarrely unable to come up with an answer, blaming his appalling lack of forthrightness on "legal matters."

And the king of South Florida late night talk radio was more interested, he said, in the purveyors of steroids than those who take the substances. The people who get the drugs to the athletes—those are the real bad guys, or at least the worst guys. Like in the cocaine or heroin trades, where the drug lords are the most reviled figures, the monsters we love to hate.

And hate them we should, for they are, no doubt, despicable. But the purveyors of steroids and the drug lords to which they are, in a sense, comparable, are to our drug problem what a headache is to a brain tumor. Yes, the headache is painful and is the most "visible" part of the problem, but it is no more than a symptom, and can even be mitigated with pain killers, while the actual problem itself, the tumor, silently devours the brain.

As long as athletes like Jason Giambi make tens of millions of dollars for playing baseball (Giambi's 2004 salary was $12.4 million, according to ESPN), many of them will do whatever they can to have an edge. And, as long as home runs will fill up stadiums, Major League Baseball will try its very best to turn a blind eye to steroid use. Given the environments talented ballplayers find themselves in since high school (or even earlier sometimes), it would be surprising if they did not use steroids, and naïve for us to expect them not to. And it would be even more naïve to not expect opportunists to instantly materialize to purvey the 'roids, since there is a significant buck to be made. The "tumor" in this case is neither the steroid junkie nor the steroid pusher, but the situation that drives them both: a society that values ballplayers more than scientists and teachers, and doesn't realize—or, even worse, doesn't really care—that much of what we've come to expect from professional athletes is simply impossible for an enhancement-free human body to produce.

I know what you're thinking: not all athletes use steroids, so why cynically dismiss steroid use as an almost inevitable consequence of our value system? Well, those athletes who are able to compete without cheating, those who have both the talent and character necessary to resist the seductive call of artificial enhancement, deserve that much more credit.

When it comes to other drugs—cocaine, heroin, ecstasy, or whatever is in vogue these days—the "tumor" is the elusive reason why so many of us succumb to drug use. We need to understand why the rich guy takes his BMW down to the 'hood to make a purchase, because without him there is no drug lord. And tell me please, exactly what is the difference between a supplier of marijuana, a drug widely used and often abused, and a supplier of alcohol, another drug widely used and often abused? There really is no difference, except in social standing, and maybe table manners.

We spend billions in a pathetically futile attempt to stop the drug trade and eradicate the drug lords, ignoring the tragic reality that although we may lessen the headache by doing so, the tumor will continue to grow, and many more and stronger headaches will develop.

How to deal with the tumor? Damn good question, to be sure, but as with the steroid issue, if we somehow suck the absurdly high dollars out of the equation, human nature will take care of the rest, and there will be no more headaches because there will no longer be tumors. Maybe a legalized drug trade is a logical first step, since the economics of the drug market would drastically change, sort of like what happened at the end of Prohibition. But I have yet to hear of a politician with the courage to make that painfully politically incorrect proposal. And, looking back at the steroid issue, it seems we have always been, and will always be, in awe of physical talent. We astonishingly treasure those with the talent to entertain us much more than those with the talent to teach us, to enrich us, or even to save us from ourselves.

I'm sure my old friend Eddie K, astute commentator on human nature and proud owner of an amazingly sharp intellect, would have much to say about this.

Walt, You Can't Be Serious!

February 19, 2005

WALTER S. MOSSBERG is one of the most respected technology writers out there, and deservedly so. I particularly admire his uncanny ability to tackle complex subjects and present them in elegant simplicity, belying his vast technical expertise while truly helping his readers understand and cope with the technology-related issues they face on a daily basis.

As befitting the enlightened purveyor of objective and succinct information that he so demonstrably is, Mr. Mossberg has traditionally recognized the unique benefits that the Macintosh platform delivers to its users. So it was with eyebrows raised in disbelief that I read his latest column, entitled "While Switching to Mac Will Improve Security, It Isn't for Everybody." While Mr. Mossberg clearly states in the column that he stands by his previous advice to Windows users that "one way out" of the virus and spyware mess that is Windows these days is to "switch to Apple's Macintosh," he also, astoundingly, says, ". . . switching to the Mac has downsides, and it isn't the best course for some groups of Windows users . . ."

Say what?

I would like to respectfully present rebuttals to the points Mr. Mossberg makes in the balance of his column, as follows:

WM: "In general, the best candidates for a switch to the Mac are those who use their computers overwhelmingly for common, mainstream consumer tasks. These include email, instant messaging and Web browsing; word processing, spreadsheets and presentations; working with photos, home videos and digital music; and playing and creating CDs and DVDs.

"The Mac is as good as Windows at these core tasks, and in many cases better. Still, you certainly shouldn't consider switching to the Mac if you are happy with Windows and you aren't much affected by viruses and spyware."

JSA: First, the tasks referred to by Mr. Mossberg as "common, mainstream computer tasks" cover about 90 percent of the things people do with their computers. And the Mac platform undoubtedly excels when applied to some of the most demanding computer tasks out there, such as professional digital image editing, professional graphics work, professional video editing, and the clustering of computers for scientific research. I'm not sure what other tasks Mr. Mossberg has in mind, but unless they involve software that simply does not exist for the Mac platform, I cannot fathom how people who use their computers for those tasks would not benefit by switching to the robust, stable, elegant Macintosh platform.

Second, when Mr. Mossberg mentions people who are "happy with Windows and . . . aren't much affected by viruses and spyware" he is referring to an extremely small subset of humanity, even taking into consideration the sneaky use of the word "much" to obfuscate the fact that there are very, very few Windows users who are not affected at all by viruses and spyware, while every single Mac user out there is living in virus- and spyware-free bliss.

WM: "Even if you aren't happy with Windows, don't consider switching to the Mac if you are resistant to learning new ways of doing things."

JSA: This amazingly logic-free statement seems to have originated someplace other than in Mr. Mossberg's finely tuned brain. Is the implication that you should stick with something you're not happy with just because you may have to adapt to a few changes if you switch? If you are "resistant to learning new ways of doing things," are you running DOS, or using pencil and paper, or drawing on cave walls? If you are so set in your ways that you would not switch from something you're not happy with to something better, well, you have more pressing issues than your choice in computer platforms.

WM: "And the standard delete key on a Mac works like the backspace key, not the delete key, in Windows. Mac desktop keyboards have a second, Windows-type delete key, but Mac laptops lack one."

JSA: When using a Mac laptop, press the Fn key while using the delete key, and presto, Mac laptops no longer "lack one."

WM: "And don't consider switching if your budget covers only the cost of the Mac itself. There will usually be extra costs. To maintain compatibility with the Windows world, you will probably want a copy of the Mac version of Microsoft Office, which isn't included by Apple.

JSA: I didn't realize that Microsoft Office was included with Windows PC's . . . oh, it's not. So why should Apple include the Mac version of Microsoft Office with their computers? This paragraph's astonishing separation from rationality truly boggles the mind!

WM: "And you may want a standard two-button, Windows-style mouse, which works fine on the Mac but isn't included."

JSA: Apple includes a high-quality one-button optical mouse with every desktop Mac, vastly superior to the plastic rubber-ball trash shipped with your run-of-the-mill Dell. And yes, if you need two buttons, you need to add $30 for an additional mouse. Breaks the bank, doesn't it?

WM: "Also, Windows users who rely on specialized business or technical software, or on custom software supplied by their employers, should be wary of switching. That's because the Mac can't run Windows software straight out of the box, and these kinds of specialized Windows programs are rarely available in Mac versions."

"You can enable a Mac to run Windows programs by buying a $240 program from Microsoft called Virtual PC. It creates a pseudo Windows computer on a portion of a Mac's hard disk. But I don't recommend relying on Virtual PC if you use multiple Windows programs frequently, because it's slow and susceptible to the same viruses and spyware as a real Windows PC."

JSA: This is a valid point. If the software you use on a daily basis only exists for Windows, you're out of luck. Virtual PC is a barely usable program, and I concur with Mr. Mossberg in recommending against it. Thing is, this becomes a catch-22. If people shy away from a better platform because there's less software developed for it, fewer developers will produce programs for that platform due to the limited user base. But this is changing.

Mr. Mossberg himself recommends that Windows users ditch the obsolete and unsafe-at-any-speed Internet Explorer and instead use the streamlined, snappy Firefox browser from the Mozilla organization. As more and more Windows users take that excellent advice (and they're doing it in droves!), Web site developers will stop cranking out Web sites that only work on the inarguably inadequate IE and will instead comply with industry standards and create sites that will work on any major browser, on any major platform. This is good for everyone, and as Web sites become more platform-agnostic, one more obstacle to free choice is blown away. Users should be able to choose the best computer and operating system out there, and not limit themselves to an inferior platform just because the software and Web sites are more plentiful.

As Web sites stop caring what browser or OS you're on, and software is developed for all major platforms, Steve Jobs's excellent BMW analogy will ring true: it doesn't really matter if the brand of car you drive has a low market share, as long as you have access to the same streets and highways as everyone else. In the past, Macs and Windows PCs used different sets of streets, but ever since Apple converted to Mac OS X, and more so with every new release of Mac OS X, Macs and Windows PCs coexist famously, and with that being the case users can freely choose what's best for them and not, as Mr. Mossberg points out, stay with Windows because they have no choice.

WM: "People who depend on their company's IT department to manage and support their home computers may find themselves locked into Windows. Most corporate computer staffs support only Windows and know little or nothing about Macs."

JSA: Again, true. But chances are that if your home computer were a Mac you just wouldn't need your company's IT department to manage and support it. Why would anyone want corporate IT people to manage their home computer anyway? And hey, if you need help with your home Mac, just call your friendly neighborhood member of the Apple Consultants Network. Since we (I'm a proud member) are not out there cleaning virus- and spyware-infested machines all day long, we'll be happy to get you up and running with your Mac home network!

WM: "Similarly, if the principal use of your home computer is to remotely link up to your company's Windows network, stay with Windows. The Mac has gotten much better at doing these remote linkups, but they are still easier on Windows."

JSA: Today it is just as easy to join a Windows network from a Mac as from a Windows PC. Yes, I'm serious. This applies remotely also. So unless you are linking up to use software that does not exist on the Mac, Mr. Mossberg's statement is simply inaccurate. If you remotely link to a Windows network to access, say, MS Office files for example, the Mac will do it easily and elegantly.

WM: "If you love Microsoft Outlook, you should also probably stick with Windows. There is no version of Outlook for the current Mac operating system. Instead, Microsoft includes an email and organizer program called Entourage in the Mac version of Office. It's similar to Outlook but just different enough to bug Outlook lovers."

JSA: True again. But does anyone truly "love" Outlook? Most people I know would "love" to be rid of it!

WM: "If you use your PC mainly for games, avoid the Mac. While there are more games for the Mac now than there were a few years back, the number still lags behind Windows badly. And the hottest computer games come out first, and sometimes exclusively, on Windows."

JSA: True. No argument here. I would refer you to my catch-22 reference . . .

WM: "People who rely heavily on financial software may be unhappy with the Mac. Microsoft Money doesn't come in a Mac version. The Mac version of Quicken isn't identical to the Windows product, and converting Windows Quicken data to the Mac is a bear. Many specialized financial-analysis and stock-trading programs aren't available for Macs."

JSA: The Mac version of Quicken lags about one version behind the Windows version, but this is by no means a deal breaker. And, as someone who has on many occasions converted Quicken for Windows data to Quicken for Mac, I would by no means call the conversion a "bear"; actually it's pretty straight-forward. There's a great cross-platform accounting solution out there, NetSuite, and if you'd like to learn more about it please let me know, since I'm a longtime user and an Alliance Partner.

WM: "If you need an ultralight laptop for traveling, you're out of luck with Apple. The Mac laptops are great, but the lightest one weighs 4.6 pounds, compared with three pounds or less on the Windows side."

JSA: If a pound or so of traveling weight is more important to you than an exquisitely designed laptop with an industrial-strength, elegant and easy to use operating system, yes, stick with the ThinkPad or VAIO.

WM: "If you use a portable music player other than Apple's iPod, or love the major subscription music services, Napster and Rhapsody, which work only on Windows, you won't be happy with a Mac."

JSA: The market has overwhelmingly rejected music subscription services, and the iPod remains the de facto standard and best portable music player out there. So, by switching to a Mac you ditch unsuccessful wannabes and retain access to the most popular music store and the often-imitated but not-yet-matched overwhelmingly world-favorite portable player. And this is somehow bad?

WM: "The bottom line is that the Mac is a great alternative for mainstream consumers doing mainstream tasks who are sick and tired of the Windows security crisis. But it isn't for everybody."

JSA: I agree with Mr. Mossberg's conclusion in a general sense, but he and I differ vastly in our determination of the groups of people for whom the Mac is not a great alternative. My bottom line is that Apple builds some of the best computers out there today, and Mac OS X is clearly the best operating system on the planet. I say this not out of fanaticism or cultism, but out of objectivity. My first ever experience with a computer was with an Apple II running Visicalc in the late '70s, After that, though, I jumped on the IBM PC bandwagon, which took me through MS-DOS, Windows 3.1, Windows 95, Windows NT, and Windows 2000 without even a look at the Macintosh platform. That is, until December 2001, when serendipity and a gentle nudge from my wonderful wife guided me toward the newly opened Apple Store at The Falls (Miami, Florida), where I was instantly seduced by a sexy and powerful titanium PowerBook coyly perched on one of their display tables.

I converted to Mac on the spot.

I've never looked back.

Although I had always been fascinated by computers, I so enjoyed working with Mac OS X that a few months after my first experience with Kyla (my new PowerBook) I became an IT Consultant, trained and certified by Apple on the Mac OS X and Mac OS X Server platforms. And all the work that I've done for my clients since then has reinforced my belief that Apple hardware and the Mac OS X operating system present the highest quality alternative in computer equipment today, bar none.

The virus/spyware quagmire that most Windows users find themselves in is probably the most compelling motivation for a switch to the Mac platform. But make no mistake, if Windows viruses and spyware were to disappear tomorrow, the switch from Windows to Mac would continue to present myriad benefits to users. Mac OS X is simply a better operating system than Windows, and as such it does what operating systems are supposed to do better than Windows does. This means it stays out of the way and allows the user to focus on his tasks. This means it allows the user to work the way she wants to work—with many applications and processes running simultaneously, with the ability to go to "sleep" at a moment's notice, and instantly "wake up" and pick up where it left off without so much as a hiccup, being able to switch from wired networking to wireless and back seamlessly. This means handling itself with stability and aplomb, and requiring to be restarted only when installing an OS update or other significant event. I don't think anyone who knows operating systems would argue this point . . . well, anyone outside of Redmond, anyway.

There are users out there who rely on certain software and Web sites that simply cannot be accessed natively with a Mac, and I wholeheartedly agree with Mr. Mossberg that Virtual PC is a dog of a program that does not present a viable solution for those users. They sadly have no choice at this time but to put up with the frustrating experience that is Windows today. However, I strongly feel that the days of Windows 90-plus-percent dominance of the personal computer are waning, and the next 5–10 years will bring healthy and much-needed diversity to the world's desktops, with Windows playing a decreased role, and Linux and Mac OS X increasing their market shares dramatically. And this diversity, as is the case with diversity in general, will benefit everyone.

In the meantime, any user who does not rely on Windows-only software or Web sites would benefit from a switch to Mac

OS X, just as a Hyundai driver would benefit from switching to BMW—except without the cost difference. Yes, there are some new things to learn, and maybe the driver will initially find himself in unfamiliar territory. But getting to know your shiny new car, putting it through its paces and exploring its many wonders are all joyous experiences. As is doing the same with your shiny new Mac.

Update

The more things change, the more they stay the same! Although much has changed since I wrote this essay a little over three years ago, the main thrust is more relevant than ever—actually so relevant that it may have become obvious, and obsolete.

If switching from Windows to the Mac was compelling in February 2005, it is darn close to irresistible today. Macs are more compatible with traditional Windows environments than ever, and through virtualization or dual-boot technology, Mac users can easily and seamlessly run any version of Windows on their Macs in the event that they absolutely need to run software that is Windows-only. Other points made my Mr. Mossberg are no longer relevant, such as the two-button mouse (Apple now ships the multi-control Mighty Mouse with every desktop Mac) and the existence of a Mac ultra-portable machine (MacBook Air, anyone?).

Today the Macintosh platform is growing exponentially, helped along by the ubiquitous iPod and, more recently, the iPhone and iPod touch, while the once-invincible Windows, in large part due to the startlingly underwhelming introduction of Windows Vista, is a stagnant platform showing signs of impending decline.

Cursive?

March 1, 2005

DURING A RECENT parent-teacher conference my son's first grade teacher casually grumbled about the hard time kids have learning the slanted and looping cursive, accustomed as they are to the boxy, straight print they've learned so far.

So I'm thinking: who came up with this cursive stuff anyway, and why should anyone have to learn it?

In the magical age of Google the first part is easy: cursive writing, or "running hand" was invented by Aldus Manutius of Venice, who for reasons known only to himself and perhaps other Venetians, departed from the old set forms of writing in a.d. 1495 and thus created all sorts of hassles for humanity thereafter.

Today, books are not printed in cursive. Computer screens do not express themselves in cursive (unless you really want them to, but you've got to be a bit eccentric to want them to). Most adults I know do not write in cursive; they either print, or scrawl stuff that looks like the output of some crazy seismometer. (I fit squarely in the second category.) Adults of my father's generation, who were drilled from childhood in an archaic method of torture referred to in hushed tones as The Palmer Method of Penmanship, are the exceptions to this rule. My father has exquisite handwriting, and can, to this day, form a row of perfect, connected ovals. I guess if there's a choice opening in the scribe market he will have an excellent shot to nab one of those coveted positions!

In the meantime, though, my father would gladly trade in his perfect ovals for a new set of typing skills, as would many others of his generation who have, as he, adopted the computer as their preferred method of expression.

So I bravely say here and now, let's eliminate the scourge of cursive writing from our schools. Let's replace it with early touch typing instruction. Let's do this today. And let's give our children a skill that they will use, appreciate, and enjoy every day of their lives, instead of wasting their time and brainpower on an archaic skill that they will never need.

Humanity 1.1

March 14, 2005

SO LET'S SAY you are presented with two different organisms of the same species, Organism A and Organism B. They differ from each other in the following ways, among others:

While Organism A is a linear, one-task-at-a-time life form, Organism B has native multitasking, multithreading capabilities. It is thus able to handle two or more different tasks, or two or more processes related to the same task, simultaneously, without material degradation in speed or quality of any of the tasks or processes. Sort of à la Mac OS X. Organism A, despite its lack of multitasking capability, often attempts to perform that function anyway, sometimes successfully bluffing, but often with disastrous end results. Sort of like the operating systems that preceded the aforementioned Mac OS X.

Organism B is vastly more tolerant of pain than Organism A, and as a result is able to handle the most difficult physical challenges faced by the species: the internal nurturing of offspring from conception, and the excruciating delivery of the offspring. The difference in pain threshold between the two organisms is so severe that it is widely believed, although impossible to verify, that if Organism A were charged with the procreation responsibilities currently handled with elegant aplomb by Organism B, the species itself would cease to exist within one generation.

With regard to their reproductive systems, Organism A's sexual function may be likened to a hard-boiled egg: simple to prepare and bring to a successful conclusion, yet abundantly satisfying. Organism B's sexual function is more like Eggs Benedict with all the trimmings: vastly more complex to prepare, difficult to properly achieve, allowing all sorts of delicious opportunities for creativity and improvisation, and end results which vary from the colossally catastrophic to the almost impossibly sublime. Or, put differently, Organism A's sexual system is a superb idea, well executed in the first effort. Organism B's is a more aggressive, grander vision, with the potential for infinitely enhanced profoundness and depth, albeit more difficult to master and, alas, with a few bugs.

There are many other differences between the organisms, and myriad efforts have been put forth to explain these differences. One such effort even theorizes that the organisms are from different planets. However, and as a specimen of Organism A this is not easy to write, the explanation is simple. Organism A is Humanity 1.0, also known as Man. Organism B is Humanity 1.1, also known as Woman. And although there is appreciable improvement in Version 1.1 versus Version 1.0, we must remember that the species itself is in no way the pinnacle of evolution we members of it like to think it is, but more a pretty crude work in progress, which hopefully will demonstrate the capacity to properly steward the planet it inhabits and the other species therein in some future version—probably around 4.0 or thereabouts.

Hardwired Honesty

March 26, 2005

TERRI SCHIAVO'S HUSBAND, Michael Schiavo, claims that his severely brain-damaged wife would choose not to receive life-prolonging medical care under her current tragic circumstances, and should therefore be allowed to die. Terri's parents disagree, accusing Michael of acting out of self-interest, since, should Terri die, Michael would be entitled to what's left of a malpractice settlement. Michael says he is willing to donate the malpractice funds to charity. Terri's parents still don't believe he is acting in the best interests of his wife, although more than 20 judges have sided with Michael since the legal wrangling over Terri's fate began in 1998. Most people agree that the person best equipped to make life-and-death decisions for another is his or her spouse. But according to Terri's parents and many others who have become fascinated by this heartbreaking case, Michael Schiavo simply cannot be trusted.

During the last few weeks, two severely brain damaged people (an infant and an elderly man) were allowed to die in Texas. In that state, doctors and hospital ethics boards are empowered to disconnect patients from life-sustaining systems if they conclude that the patient's condition is hopeless, even over the objections of family members. Interestingly, these powers were granted to doctors and hospitals by Texas' Advance Directives Act, signed into law in 1999 by then governor George W. Bush. Seems like a good idea: doctors have both the knowledge and the objective standpoint necessary to best make those impossibly difficult decisions. Seems like a good idea, that is, until you listen to the attorney for the people who were allowed to die. It is his point of view, you see, that the doctors and hospital ethics boards who decided to let the infant and the elderly man die were acting in the economic interest of the hospital, not the best interest of the patients. The doctors and ethics boards, the attorney argues, simply cannot be trusted.

So it all boils down to trust, or, really, the lack thereof. We have law enforcement and courts because we cannot be trusted. We have the Department of Homeland Security because we can't be trusted. We have armed forces because we can't be trusted. We have religion, in part, because we can't be trusted to do the right thing of our own volition. We have safes and locks because we cannot be trusted. We have licenses, certificates, and other documents of proof because we cannot be trusted. Seems like human beings—whether they be military personnel guarding Iraqi prisoners at Abu Ghraib, priests interacting with prepubescent boys, corporate executives planning financial strategies, teenagers presenting identification at bars, or many of us preparing our tax returns—can be counted on to do the wrong thing with alarming frequency. So we develop complex and astoundingly expensive systems first to deter dishonesty and then to pathetically attempt to correct things when the deterrents inevitably fail.

Lieutenant Commander Data, an android memorably played by Brent Spiner in the outstanding television series *Star Trek: The Next Generation*, was programmed by his creator, Dr. Noonien Soong, not to lie or deceive. Can you imagine life if humans were endowed with Data's hardwired honesty? It literally boggles the mind, simply because much of the infrastructure we have built on our planet would become instantly obsolete. So much is built on the lamentably accurate assumption that people will lie that if they suddenly don't, everything would change. Honesty, held up as one of the universal principles of humanity, is universally cast aside with astonishing ease by the same people who ostensibly revere it.

When they think they can get away with it, that is.

Hardwired honesty. Lieutenant Data got it in 2338. Maybe we'll get it in a future version of the Homo Sapiens Operating System (appropriately, H-SOS). I'll put in a feature request. Don't hold your breath.

Update

On March 31, 2005, just a few days after I wrote this essay, Terry Schiavo died at 9:05 A.M. with her husband Michael at her side. Her parents and siblings were not there, though, because Michael had banished them from her room during Terry's final hours. Terry Schiavo's epitaph reads: "Schiavo / Theresa Marie / Beloved Wife / Born December 3, 1963 / Departed this Earth February 25, 1990 / At Peace March 31, 2005."

What's in a Name

April 16, 2005

JESUS CHRIST IS, no doubt, the star of the New Testament. Yes, there are other characters, many of them important: a virgin, saints, apostles, and I'm sure still others I've never even heard of. But the Son of God, that product of pleasure-free procreation, the turner of water into wine, Mr. Resurrection himself, is, unquestionably, the leading man.

Meanwhile, according to most estimates approximately 56 percent of our country's population is Protestant and 28 percent is Catholic. Therefore, a whopping 84 percent of Americans have at least some degree of belief in the New Testament.

U.S. Census Bureau figures from the 1990 census indicate that the most frequently occurring first name in the United States is James, a name shared by over 3 percent of our nation's male population. James is closely followed by John, Robert, and Michael, with William closing out the top five. These top five first names cover over 12.3 percent of the males in this country.

I know what you're thinking: OK, so what? Well, please continue to bear with me for a bit.

As you might have guessed, the top female first name in the United States is Mary. Number 2 is Patricia, followed by Linda, Barbara, and Elizabeth. Interestingly, the top ten male first names cover over 23.1 percent of all males in the U.S., while the top ten female first names only cover 10.7 percent of U.S. females. Apparently parents get a bit more creative when choosing monikers for their daughters, while they tend to stick with the tried and true when naming their sons.

You may ask, so, what's with the names, and what does that have to do with the New Testament and our friend the Savior? As it turns out, patient reader, if you look for Jesus on the list of the 100 most commonly occurring first names among males in the United States, your search will sadly be in vain, for the name Jesus is ranked 129th on the list!

Yes, 129th! That's behind Bradley, Melvin, and Chad! More people chose to name their son Travis than to honor him with the name of many people's Lord and Savior! Only 15 in 10,000 males in the U.S. are named Jesus, while 331 in 10,000 are named James. That's 20 times more Jameses than Jesuses, folks.

To make matters even more interesting, despite the fact that fewer than 2 in 1,000 Americans choose to name their son Jesus, over 26 in 1,000 name their daughter after Jesus' chaste mom, the Virgin Mary! So, approximately 17 times more people choose to name their child after the mother of the central figure in Christianity than they do after the central figure himself. Also, you do have the names Christopher (11th on the male list) and Christine (43rd on the female list), obviously somehow connected with the man from Nazareth, but again, no top-100 finish for the Nazarene himself.

So, in conclusion, Christians tend overwhelmingly to name their sons in honor of biblical figures. They inexplicably, however, eschew the top guy. Sort of like naming your phone company WatsonSouth, or your capital city Adams, or your car company Lieutenant Motors. (I know, that last one doesn't really work, but you get the idea.) Why is this? If I knew, it wouldn't have stuck to the sifter!

Fairness in an Unfair World

May 10, 2005

"T HAT'S NOT FAIR!"
How many times have we, as parents, heard those words wailed out by children on the verge of a spectacular crying fit? And, as parents, we have a couple of choices in terms of how to respond. We can:
  A. Try to "correct" the situation, and make it "fair."
  B. Explain to our offspring that the universe may be many things, but fair, alas, is simply not one of them.

Of course, we will almost certainly go with option A because, as human beings, we seem to have a built-in, hard-wired yearning for fairness—even though it is generally as unachievable as, say, world peace, or even a spyware-free Windows environment. And the problem seems to be that our hard-wired yearning for fairness is more than offset by our propensity to do the wrong thing: to take advantage of any situation where we have the upper hand, as long as we can get away with it.

So we attempt to make college and graduate school admissions fair by coming up with all sorts of standardized tests: SAT, GMAT, LSAT, FCAT, and so on. But then Mr. Kaplan comes along, happy to help your kid perform better on those tests—for a tidy sum, of course. "Higher score guaranteed—or your money back," shouts the purveyor of academic nirvana. So kids whose families can afford it will perform better on those tests. Unfair? Of course! But it turns out that some of the questions on the tests assume familiarity with concepts that may be commonplace in the estate or subdivision, but not in the 'hood or barrio. So the tests were unfair to begin with, even before the astonishing absurdity of allowing some kids to gain a clear advantage by taking a preparatory course. So yes, fairness is good, but if we can give our kid an edge . . . well, fairness is not so important anyway, right?

So we were grossly unfair to certain groups of people in the past. Enter Affirmative Action, a noble attempt to right previous wrongs. Let's be unfair to certain groups of people now to somehow make up for our past unfairness to others. So does this mean that we will, in a few years, be unfair to the groups we were unfair with originally, to make up for the fact that we are now being unfair to other groups? When will it end?

But Affirmative Action and college admission tests are but the minor leagues of "making things fair." The major leagues? Of course: the concept of heaven and hell. Since good things happen to bad people and bad things happen to good people, and that isn't fair, let's say that good people, no matter how much they suffer during their life, will eventually end up in eternal ecstasy while bad people, no matter how much they enjoy their earthly existence, will eventually find themselves forever toiling away in unspeakable agony. In one fell swoop, all the unfairness is gone! Children born to insurmountable, miserable poverty; good people stricken with horrible diseases; children orphaned by accidents, war, crime; parents left childless by the irresponsible acts of drunk drivers . . . guess what? It's OK because, in the end, heaven and hell make it all fair.

So why does the ingenious contrivance of heaven and hell promote injustice? Because, you see, the people who came up with it didn't leave well enough alone. They built a back door! If you're a sorry, despicable excuse for a human being, don't despair: the gates of heaven can open for you too! All you need is to: (Catholic version) confess your sins, repent, and do penance; (Jewish version) participate in the once-a-year Day of Atonement; (catch-all version) establish a personal relationship with your Savior. So there we are, right back to square one: even if you're a dues-paying member of the H&H club, life is still grossly unfair, because bad people can wind up in the same kingdom of eternal bliss as good people, as long as they "handle" things in the end. Finding one of those people next to you while basking in the ecstasy of heaven must feel like when you find out the guy in the seat next to you on the 757 to New York paid $125 for his round trip ticket, while you paid $800! Talk about unfair!

So life is inherently unfair, and the more we try to force it to be fair the more we muck it up and make it worse. So what's the answer? Let's just pretend we're a colony of ants, going about our merry way. Once in a while, all sorts of strange looking huge objects appear above us out of nowhere, and crush many of us to death for absolutely no reason but that we were scurrying about in the wrong place at the wrong time. Why did some of us get crushed while others continued scurrying, some of them literally millimeters from an unfortunate colleague? Since we, as human beings, understand the nature of the occurrence, we realize that the catastrophe that befell some of the ants was in no way related to their actions while here on earth. The sneaker was going to crush those hapless insects, and no last-minute absolution or quick Hail Mary was going to stop it. A bad thing happened to many ants—some of them good ants, some of them bad ants. And damn it, that was unfair!

Fill in the Blanks—NOT

May 30, 2005

IT IS SCIENTIFIC fact that nature abhors a vacuum, and will do what it possibly can to somehow fill it. Likewise, our minds seem to be conditioned to fill gaps in our knowledge. Just as nature detests empty space, our brains try to explain things, even if they need to suspend logic to do so, to avoid lack of knowledge or empty space of the mind. So we take what we know and extrapolate it to cover what we don't know, sometimes with astonishing disregard for common sense.

The ancient Greeks and Romans explained the parts of their world that they did not understand using intricate mythology. Today, the world's religions do pretty much the same. Fascinatingly, we are convinced that a belief in one God is somehow more advanced, or civilized, than a belief in many gods. Interesting, since there is about as much evidence, or, more accurately, lack thereof, for either belief, as well as for any other theory anyone can come up with.

The truth is, we simply don't know. And not knowing is somehow more disturbing to most people than filling the gap with logic-free concoctions that brazenly attempt to explain things, fail miserably, and cover their failure by asking adherents to use faith instead of reason, to feel guilt instead of disbelief. Just like the ancient Greeks and Romans, when we attempt to explain the utterly unknown, we do so by extrapolating what we do know, using the paradigms of the world around us to make sense of that which lies above our understanding. And this may be a laughable exercise in futility if what we cannot explain today lies so far beyond our current understanding that we lack the framework with which to even attempt an explanation.

While filling in the blanks of understanding is a necessary trait of our minds, and we would probably not survive without it, it also creates things like racism, stereotyping, and closed minds, and hinders open investigation. Since our minds try to take what we know and apply it to what we don't, we have a difficult time thinking "outside the box," or having an open mind. When we meet someone different from ourselves, instead of granting the person a clean slate, we immediately begin making assumptions based on what we can see, or the first things we hear. Our mind extrapolates its current knowledge, which is a dangerous thing if that current knowledge is based on prejudicial hearsay, or even on an isolated bad experience. No doubt, ignorance is the food that sustains prejudice, and knowledge its poison.

What is needed here is a Max OS X-style preference pane, with a checkbox entitled "Turn Off Extrapolation," which when checked would stop our brain from attempting to fill in the blanks with items based on its knowledge store and allow us to objectively fill the vacuums with a completely open mind. Perhaps the preference pane would also include "Clear Brain Cache" and "Stop Autocompletion" checkboxes, so that we could take a fresh look at things that come our way, and not try to fill in the details with prior experiences.

Maybe that will be one of the features of Humanity 1.1. No, wait a minute, that version was already released (please see "Humanity 1.1" on page 29).

Maybe 1.2?

Halitosis

July 17, 2005

I RECENTLY FOUND myself trapped for five hours in seat 21H of an American Airlines 767 next to a man with a severe halitosis problem. Yes, dear reader, the man had astonishingly bad breath. And every time he opened his mouth, even just slightly, not to talk, but to breathe, I got a full whiff of air of a putrid quality difficult to describe, but easy to recreate in my mind as I write about it. As the jam-packed cross-country flight progressed and I bravely endured the assault on my senses, I realized that the repulsive odor emanating from the man's mouth served to identify the air that so viciously sprang from it . . . and that was not necessarily a bad thing.

Think of it: I knew for a fact that I was inhaling that which he was exhaling because of its foul, sui generis scent. Therefore, logic would dictate that every time any of us sits next to someone else on an airplane, most of what we breathe in is what they breathe out—except that most of the time our neighbor's commendable oral hygiene causes odorless exhalations. We're still subjecting our lungs to the waste byproduct of her breathing process, but we don't realize it because the waste does not smell.

Judging from my protractedly unpleasant journey, most of the air that we breathe when on an airplane contains germs, microbes, bacteria, and who knows what else, all coming from those around us. Yet, in the overwhelming majority of cases, our bodies take in all of that abuse and deal with it so efficiently and transparently that we never even give it a second thought. Except when, for reasons unknown to mortals, our bodies succumb to the attacks of those germs and fall sick.

It seems so obvious: the main objective of medicine should be to fully understand the nature of the human immune system, and to learn to work with it to prevent disease! If we would learn to tap into the secrets of our bodies' miraculous defense mechanisms, and understand how to nurture and strengthen them, we would be able to stop disease before it starts, and save millions of lives and billions of dollars!

But hey, apparently understanding the amazing human immune system and helping it prevent disease just doesn't present an economically feasible model to the Pfizers and GlaxoSmithKlines of the world. No, that sort of thing lies squarely in the jurisdiction of people whom members of the traditional medical establishment would call kooky Asians, herb hippies, and, of course, the P.T. Barnums of alternative medicine. Big Pharma can't afford to lose its focus on keeping cashcow cancer and dialysis patients alive (without worrying about figuring out why their kidneys fail to begin with, or why their bodies suddenly turn on themselves), and helping people lose weight without really trying. How can we expect doctors to spend time understanding our bodies' disease-fighting mechanisms when there are women today forced to go through life with, egad, small breasts? *[Author's note: Most men, the editorial staff at sifterstickers.com certainly included, find small, well-proportioned breasts just as sexy if not more so than large breasts. Just thought you should know, dear female reader.]* Doctors are lining up to make sure that every man has a full head of hair until the day he drops dead, that every woman's facial muscles are nicely paralyzed into full loss of expression (and wrinkles, of course). And, lest we forget, drug company coffers are overflowing with cash parted with gladly by men hoping to find out how it feels to have a four-hour erection.

A bit harsh? Maybe. But there's no doubt that traditional medicine today would serve humanity better by focusing more on preventing disease than on dealing with it after the fact. Isn't an ounce of prevention worth a pound of cure? And yes, too many of our resources are being squandered on frivolous, superficial endeavors that demonstrate all too clearly our obsession with youth and our overwhelming concern with appearance.

Is capitalism failing us here? No. Capitalism is but a mirror we hold before us. And the mirror is not responsible if we don't like what we see.

WWDK

August 28, 2005

ALBERT EINSTEIN ONCE said, "Science is what you know. Philosophy is what you don't know." Wise words, to be sure, but their wisdom is lost on many people, particularly those involved in the euphemistically named "intelligent design" movement.

One clear area of distinction between What We Know (WWK) and What We Don't Know (WWDK) is that we can all agree on WWK. No one can reasonably dispute scientific fact. WWDK, on the other hand, is fair game for speculation and interpretation—and thus conflicting views. And that is why, dear reader, although I take no issue whatsoever with believers in intelligent design (ID), I take serious issue with those who feel that ID belongs in science class.

For those unfamiliar with the ID concept, it is an updated, polished version of creationism. Its proponents purport to accept evolution, unlike their creationist brethren. But the ID crowd adds a twist: the actual development of primitive life initially and human beings eventually could not, ID believers maintain, have happened without some kind of guidance from above, read

God. So, the fact that life somehow developed from the primordial soup is part of WWK. Exactly how and why it happened are firmly in the WWDK camp. ID forms part of a presumptuous subset of WWDK: What Must Have Been (WMHB). Exactly how did life emerge from the primordial soup? Science says, simply, at this time we don't know. ID says, it "must" have been God. Our survey says . . . (sorry, again too much '70s TV).

WWDK is the gap that faith, philosophy, and religion step in to fill. And fill it they do, with each faith having its own version of WMHB. Cool so far. But no matter how strong the faith, WMHB is still part of WWDK, and WWDK must be kept separate from WWK. Like Superman and Kryptonite. Like vinegar and baking soda. Like relationship George and independent George. Like the Mac and Intel processors. (Oops, strike that last one!). Crossing the sacrosanct line between WWK and WWDK by teaching a specific version of WMHB as if it were WWK in public school science class is tantamount to state-sponsored religion, and slaps religious freedom hard in the face. How can a family practice their faith at home if another faith's WMHB is taught as scientific fact to their children?

I have no problem with, and actually would strongly encourage, teaching different versions of WMHB in school as what they are: faith-based beliefs. In fact, teaching students about differing versions of WMHB encourages open minds and the understanding of other religions and cultures. If children grow up understanding that different people have different beliefs, and that until we know the facts all beliefs are just as valid, maybe, just maybe, mutual respect and understanding will replace much of the bigotry and ignorance-based hate we see today. But for that to happen, we all must agree that WWDK is just that, and that the "we" in WWDK means everyone. We must resist the temptation to impose our own beliefs on others, no matter how strong our own faith, or lack thereof. And in order not to impose our own beliefs, we must actually acknowledge that the beliefs of others are just as valid as our own. Given our species' track record in this regard, I think there's a better chance that I'll be asked to replace the Diesel at center for the Heat this year. Or that Apple will ship a multi-button mouse.

Well, maybe we have a shot after all!

Update

Sometimes things that seem wildly implausible at one point in time simply happen, and are subsequently taken for granted. Like Apple finally shipping the Mighty Mouse a few weeks before I wrote this essay, or Apple moving to the Intel chip in early 2006. But will our inability to respect the beliefs of others suddenly be replaced with tolerance and understanding some day, like the MacBook Pro suddenly replaced the PowerBook G4 in January 2006? Or will human tolerance be as elusive as that Heat center position is to a 5'9", 46-year-old who can jump about 4 inches on a good day? I'm hoping for the former, but if I were a betting man the odds would have to be pretty steep for me to put any money on it!

The Drive to Contrive

November 5, 2005

THE INCREDIBLE HULK is a sprawling green monster of a roller coaster, whose tracks snake their way above the Islands of Adventure theme park in Orlando. Hard to believe, but I actually rode this beast once, to prove to my roller-coaster-loving daughter that I wasn't as much of a chicken as her previously unsuccessful attempts to get me on similar so-called attractions would seem to indicate. My experience on The Hulk that day may best be illustrated by the first words uttered by the 12-year-old kid on the other side of me when the ride was over, with all the knowing condescension a pre-teenager can muster: "Sir, this was your first time, right?"

Truth is, I'd rather be subjected to extensive root canal work than to ever experience The Incredible Hulk again. And that's certainly not because I'm fond of the dental chair, as the beautiful and talented Mirtha Amador, DDS, would certainly attest. It's because, in my view, mortal danger is clearly something to be avoided, not something to be contrived. I simply do not enjoy feeling scared for my life.

And my discomfort with risk of life and limb extends to others. Watching a tightrope walker or trapeze artist brings me stress, not pleasure. The fact that others enjoy watching people risk their lives is as baffling to me as the fact that others enjoy feeling as if they are risking their own lives. I'm convinced that if any aliens have infiltrated our planet and are secretly observing us, they are baffled as well. For I know of no other member of the animal kingdom that apparently does not experience enough fear from real-life dangers, and thus simulates additional dangerous situations simply for fun.

Baffling or not, however, the fact remains, a large percentage of us actually enjoy the "thrill" of danger, the invigorating high that comes from knowing (or thinking) that we may be killed or seriously injured during the next few seconds. Why is this? Could it be that our ancestors' lives were riddled with danger to such an extent that their bodies adjusted by thriving on fear, instead of succumbing to it? And those who thrived on fear survived, passing along their danger-loving characteristic? And so, since our lives apparently aren't riddled with enough danger anymore (feel free to smirk here), we need to contrive it to satisfy our thrill-seeking needs?

Or maybe the reason we humans seem to enjoy the exhilaration that comes with exposure to danger is that without that seemingly irrational characteristic, exploration and many other kinds of progress would be impossible. If Alan Sheppard isn't willing to cram himself inside a tiny space capsule perched on a monstrous Saturn V rocket, knowing full well that the Saturn has a darn good chance of exploding into a million pieces, we have no space program. And so on.

But does this mean that the same human characteristic that drove Chuck Yeager to push the envelope drives my daughter to ride The Hulk? Do John Glenn and Neil Armstrong share this characteristic with *Fear Factor* contestants? Would your average amusement park thrill seeker make a good firefighter? Is the capacity to thrive under truly dangerous conditions the same, or even related to, the attraction to contrived, fake danger?

I'm not sure about the answers to those questions. But I can tell you that personally, I find no valid reason to supplement the myriad hazards that the universe throws my way with simulated hazards. So to the condescending 12-year-old I say yes, kid, this was my first time. And hopefully my last.

Just Scan, Man

December 1, 2005

O NCE IN A while, a product works so intuitively and efficiently that you find yourself wanting another person to be in the room with you the first time you see it perform, just so you don't feel like a complete lunatic when you exclaim, "Wow! Did you see that?" And, when the product happens to be a low-profile office item that's not very well known, a Sifter Stickers essay seems warranted, although product reviews are most definitely not standard Sifter Stickers fare. So, instead of running out of my office and bringing people in from the street to show them my new Fujitsu ScanSnap scanner, I'll rave about it here.

A few months back I decided to make our Miami office totally paperless. Granted, "paperless" is a relative term; you will find plenty of blank paper at 4961 SW 75th Avenue, as well as a couple of printers and a copier. However, you will not find traditional files and folders. We created an electronic "file cabinet," established a logical folder hierarchy, and decided that May 1 would be NMP-day (no more paper, of course). And since that day I have done more scanning than I ever would have believed possible.

Although part of our strategy in becoming paperless consisted of establishing electronic-only relationships with most of our vendors and customers, there is still much content that shows up at our office in the form of paper. Most customers still send paper checks in payment for services, for example, and these checks must be deposited, paper deposit slips filled out, and copies kept. Many vendors simply do not have either the capability or the desire to email invoices or statements, and continue to use paper. So scan we must, and scan we do.

Being a small office, we did not have the budget to invest the cost of a small car for one of those refrigerator-sized behemoths that scans 1000 pages in 5 seconds and makes you a cup of decaf espresso while you wait. I had recently purchased an intermediate machine, in the $600 range, for a client, and it worked pretty well, but it was still a bit dear for our modest operation. So we made do with a $120 model, a flatbed scanner with an add-on automatic sheet feeder. It worked OK, but even for a single-page job you could easily enjoy a nice cup of coffee between the time you loaded the paper and the time the scan job was done. Even worse, the configuration had to be reset for different types of scan jobs. For example, you could configure the machine for one-sided, black-and-white scans in low resolution, say, to scan in a vendor invoice. But if the next thing you wanted to scan was a customer check, for which you'd like to scan both sides in color, you would need to go back into the scanner's settings, reconfigure, and then scan. It was enough to make you want to go back to paper!

We decided to demote our original scanner from its starring role to that of an occasionally used understudy, in favor of a new model, priced close to $200. And yes, there was certainly improvement, but I sort of felt like the princess who kisses a frog, which spectacularly becomes . . . a really good-looking frog. Not exactly what was hoped for. So we plodded along with our "improved" scanner for a couple of months, until, in the midst of a particularly tedious scanning session, I suddenly realized that hey, I bill by the hour, and when I'm scanning, I'm not billing! So, for the third time in about as many months I found myself "in the market" for a scanner. And luckily—with two strikes against me—on the third pitch, instead of swinging at another one in the dirt I connected on a rocket to the upper deck.

The first thing I liked about the Fujitsu ScanSnap was that one of their models is geared specifically for the Macintosh platform. I had found that in many cases scanner manufacturers ship their products with excellent drivers for Windows, and reluctantly include the Mac software as a redheaded afterthought. While those scanners work with relative pep on Windows, they are absolute dogs on my platform of choice, Mac OS X. So I decided to go for it all, and order the diminutive, elegant ScanSnap for about $400, bringing my total investment in scanners for the year to an astounding $720. But after just a few weeks of enjoying the ScanSnap, I can honestly say that I would have happily paid $720 for the ScanSnap alone (if you happen to work for the Fujitsu marketing department, kindly ignore that last remark.), and so what if I have a couple of ugly-looking doorstops masquerading as scanners in my office?

The ScanSnap is extremely small, taking up about as much space on a desk as a 12" iBook. Although I knew the machine's dimensions when I purchased it, this thing is so small that opening the box it almost felt like they forgot to pack the scanner. You feed it vertically, which is to say you place the paper (up to 50 sheets) in its feeder almost perpendicular to the desk. You press a button. And forget about going anywhere—before you can even step away from the machine, the job is done.

As you press the button, the ScanSnap takes about one-tenth of a second to think about it, and then the paper just flows right through it. (An analogy involving goose excrement comes to mind, but will not be used here in the interest of decorum.) If you have multiple pages, the ScanSnap gobbles them up like there's no tomorrow. And, although you can configure the ScanSnap manually, in Automatic mode the scanner will, in an awesome display of technology done right, determine on its own whether to scan both sides of the page, and whether to scan in color. Let me put this a different way. If you feed the ScanSnap a black-and-white document that is blank on one side, you will get a one-page scanned image of the printed side of the document. If the original document is printed on both sides, you will get a two-page scanned image, one page for each side. And, mind you, the ScanSnap takes exactly the same amount of time to do its job either way. A far cry from my scanner number one, which (I am not making this up) actually pulled the paper back through its feeder, and pushed it through a second time in order to scan the other side. If it had been configured for two-sided scanning beforehand, of course.

Color? No problem. The ScanSnap will automatically scan in color when the original is in color. And yes, sports fans, if you feed it a two-page document consisting of, as an example, a one-sided, black and white page, and a two-sided color page, it will, amazingly, produce a three-page scanned image, with one page in black and white and the other two in color. The first time my ScanSnap performed this astonishing feat I had to contain myself from running outside and dragging an unsuspecting FedEx guy into my office to witness this glorious display.

The one thing the ScanSnap does not do is scan multi-page documents with different-sized originals. You must scan different sized originals separately. But that is a minor quibble, barely worth mentioning, really. In general, the Fujitsu ScanSnap simply functions exactly as you would want it to. So scanning a 30-page, double-sided original is no longer interminable drudgery. It is actually fun.

And that, my friend, is exactly what technology is for.

Update

Newer ScanSnap models do scan multi-page documents with different-sized originals. Will wonders never cease?

Hephaestus

December 7, 2005

IMAGINE, IF YOU will, that you are an alien from the planet Hephaestus, in the Beta Quadrant, sent to Earth to study these beings that call themselves humans. Hephaestus, like its neighbor Vulcan, is a planet where logic reigns supreme. And although your ears are not pointy, thank you, you do tend to raise your right eyebrow and thoughtfully mutter the word "fascinating" when witnessing irrational behavior.

I wonder what you would think about the gotta-pee radio car dealer commercial guy?

For those of you not familiar with this highly technical term coined seconds ago by your crack Sifter Stickers staff, the gotta-pee radio car dealer commercial guy is the guy who recites boilerplate legal mumbo-jumbo at the end of every car dealer radio commercial, and happens to really, and I mean really, need to go to the restroom every time he reads his lines. For how else could you possibly explain the speed at which he reads them? I mean, the law requires these words to be spoken, ostensibly so that innocent bystanders inadvertently subjected to car dealer radio commercials understand certain important facts about the products featured in the commercials. But they are read at a speed that makes it impossible for anyone, with the possible exception of Lieutenant Commander Data, to understand even one word. So, the only logical explanation is that the man has got to pee, and now! Fascinating!

The gotta-pee radio car dealer commercial guy is related to another Hephaestian eyebrow-raising earthly phenomenon, the Pinocchio docs. Another recently coined, highly technical term, "Pinocchio docs" refers to documents that instantly make flagrant liars out of those who interact with them. And every human who, when installing software, is confronted by a license agreement that must be agreed to in order to continue with the installation, instantly becomes a flagrant liar by clicking on the link that says, quite unequivocally, that she has read the agreement, understands it, and agrees to abide by it. Clearly she has done nothing of the sort, and neither has anyone else who has, somewhat guiltily perhaps, clicked on that button. Had we been afflicted with Pinocchio's telltale nasal dysfunction, computer repair shops all over the world would be overrun by LCD screens and CRT monitors with a crack right in the middle, caused by a rapidly growing facial appendage. Again, fascinating!

So, the gotta-pee guy reads information that must be disclosed in a manner not understandable to those to whom the information must be disclosed. And no one actually reads Pinocchio docs, yet everyone acknowledges not only that they read them, but also that they understand them and will abide by them. Your right eyebrow is getting quite a workout!

During your long trip back to Hephaestus, you ponder all sorts of questions: Is human society overrun by inordinately zealous lawyers? Do humans simply not trust each other at all, and protect themselves from each other by requiring all sorts of legal warnings they don't appear to heed? If no one understands gotta-pee guy, and no one reads Pinocchio docs, do they actually serve the purpose they were created to serve? Why don't the people who require radio commercial disclosures require that they be presented in understandable fashion? You conclude that, for humans, reality doesn't really matter, as long as their attorneys tell them that their posterior is covered.

Back on Hephaestus you present your findings in a crowded auditorium. And five hundred eyebrows go up in unison. Fascinating indeed!

On the Brink

January 2, 2006

RECENTLY, UPON ENTERING my office, I was aggressively greeted by the odor of raw sewage. So I headed to the bathroom, logically concluding that the stench had to originate there. Yet the bathroom was absolutely sparkling. A veritable reek-o-rama with no apparent cause. I did notice one thing that was out of the ordinary, though. The water level in the toilet was a bit below where I thought I remembered it. I absently made a mental note of that detail as something to look into in the future, but in no way did I connect it to the malodorous atmosphere that had invaded ESI headquarters.

So I called upon a good friend of mine, who happens to be as knowledgeable about plumbing as I am ignorant (and that, dear reader, makes him extremely knowledgeable). Astoundingly, the first question he asked when he heard that our normally sweet-smelling office had acquired the distinct aroma of the aft lavatory of a 767 after a transatlantic flight was hey, is the water level in the toilet below normal?

"OK, now how the fuck did you know that?" was my reply.

Well, it turns out that the only thing separating us (and I mean all of us) from the pungent bouquet of Eau d'Excrement is an inch or so of water! If the water level in any toilet drops just a bit, air from the pipes below will escape its underworld prison and flow freely into the outside world, causing a major stinking disaster!

And the thin, fragile layer of water that is the difference between a pleasant aroma and a repugnant stench is the perfect metaphor for all of the other paper-thin layers that exist between normality and catastrophe in our lives. Layers like each of the thousands of complex systems that must work perfectly to accomplish the miracle of a commercial airline flight. Like the constant pumping of our hearts, the processing of toxins by our livers, and the millions of other processes taking place with absolute precision inside our bodies every second. Like the attention to the road of the driver behind us on I-95. Like the precise orbit of the earth around the sun.

The lives of ants are totally subject to our whims: if we decide to take a walk, a hundred ants peacefully living in a sidewalk crack a few steps from our front door don't get to live another day. The catastrophes that befall humanity seem just as arbitrary, just as random.

So we replaced our toilet with one that was able to maintain the water level where it should. And the offensive odors of the underworld were once again banished to their caves, where they will lurk once again, alongside all their demon disaster brethren, waiting patiently for their next day in the sun. Our next day of darkness. May the layers hold.

Breakfast of Champions

January 19, 2006

MY MATERNAL GRANDFATHER Joe was, by any measure, a unique individual. Some referred to him as a slightly eccentric. Others were harsher, thinking him a bit wacky. But all agreed, without exception, that Joe was an extraordinarily wise man, generous to a fault and with a heart the size of a small planet. Joe was, no doubt, just slightly ahead of his time, to use Panasonic's terrific tag line.

Nutrition was one of Joe's areas of self-proclaimed, yet undisputed, expertise. Among other maverick stances regarding the business of eating, during the mid-seventies Joe decided that breakfast, being the most important meal of the day, should include foods such as chicken, beef, and liver. And this thinking trickled down to our home, where for a short but glorious time we would wake up to a wonderful meal featuring a small steak, or a drumstick and thigh or two. Our forward-thinking breakfasts faded away after a year or two, and we reverted to more traditional morning fare. But my family's short-term foray into non-traditional breakfast foods flipped some kind of switch in my brain, which left me forever open minded about what to eat for breakfast.

Which brings me to the Sifter Sticker in question: what, exactly, are the criteria used to determine appropriate breakfast food in our culture? Why are lunch and dinner fair game for almost any food, while breakfast unfairly is limited to a certain, seemingly haphazard, collection of edibles? What do pancakes and scrambled eggs have in common, that, say, a tuna sandwich lacks? What is it about cereal that makes it "breakfast" cereal? Why is an Egg McMuffin appropriate for breakfast, and a Big Mac inappropriate? Hash browns are OK for breakfast; French fries are not. How absurdly arbitrary is that?

Yet everyone seems to submissively accept these strange rules. Continuing with McDonald's as our example, the restaurant (yes, I use the term loosely) actually "switches" from breakfast to lunch at 10:30 A.M., changing its entire menu in the process. And pity the poor soul who wanders in a bit late and wants a sandwich made with English muffins and eggs. No, the Breakfast Nazi says, only buns and hamburger patties for you!

When it comes to unconventionality, I will never be in the same league as my grandfather Joe. Yet, as far as breakfast foods are concerned, I have for many years eschewed the prevalent in favor of the instinctive. I'll take some tuna and crackers, a turkey sandwich, or sushi left over from the night before over eggs and bacon any day of the week. Especially the sushi. And I do it with a grateful nod to that long-gone but by no means forgotten Titan of free thought, my grandfather Joe.

Water and Diamonds

January 29, 2006

IF YOU'VE TAKEN a course in economics you may be familiar with the diamonds vs. water example: water, a substance we would literally die without, is inexpensive. Jewelry-grade diamonds have no inherent value and yet are extremely expensive. The example is used to illustrate the laws of supply and demand; water is plentiful, thus inexpensive, while diamonds are scarce (the alleged machinations of the DeBeers family to enhance this scarcity are far beyond the scope of this essay) and thus expensive.

One could draw a similar analogy using the Florida Marlin's phenom left-handed pitcher Dontrelle Willis, (diamond) versus your average elementary school teacher (water). The reason the D-train makes millions while doing nothing of real value to society while a teacher, arguably serving one of society's most important purposes, can barely make ends meet, is that Dontrelle's talents are rare, while, the analogy goes, anyone can teach fourth-grade math. Now, I vigorously take issue with this supposed logic; in my view teaching is like making love: although anyone can do it, precious few can do it well.

Thing is, for reasons better explained by trained psychologists, we are willing to pay significant money to watch Willis display his talents. And that makes his skills highly marketable, and those who pay the lefty and his ilk unfathomable amounts of money do so because it is a good investment; they make unfathomable amounts of money off of Dontrelle's talent. And that is what capitalism is all about—or is it?

Going back to our fourth-grade math teacher, he makes a pittance because no one is willing to pay anything to watch him work, and, using the public school system as our example, the people who benefit from his services don't even pay for the experience, at least not directly. However, since our elected representatives decide how much of our tax dollars are allocated to public education, it may be said that those decisions, at least roughly, reflect our own values.

As I write this, the Marlins are involved in all sorts of negotiations with the City of Miami and Miami-Dade County involving the use of public funds to finance, at least partially, a new baseball stadium in order to keep the major league baseball team in South Florida. Negotiations seem to break down every week, only to be resuscitated, but as recently as two weeks ago Miami-Dade County had already pledged $138 million (mostly financed by taxing Sunshine State tourists) toward a $420 million, retractable-roof facility (Miami Herald, 12/9/05). Yes, $138 million. To try to prevent a profitable business from leaving town by investing public funds in a facility which will help the team (did I mention that the team is a private, for-profit, enterprise?) presumably make more money here than in Las Vegas, or wherever else it threatens to go.

So, even though we all know that our children are lagging behind those in other countries as far as education is concerned, our elected officials, presumably reflecting our own values, are willing to squander $138 million on yet another South Florida sports facility. Remember, this is a city where there are two indoor arenas literally within shouting distance of each other, with another about 30 miles away in neighboring Broward County. We have a relatively new football stadium, adequate for baseball. South Florida needs another sports facility like Bill Gates needs food stamps, but that shouldn't stop anyone from building one if they feel it would be a good investment—as long as they pay for it themselves. I have no beef with the Florida Marlins, and hope they wind up staying with us for years to come. But city and county governments have about as much business paying for sports arenas as they do paying for a new office to house my own business. Which is to say none.

So the Sifter Stickers staff would like to make a proposal. With regard to using $138 million of our county's funds to help finance a stadium for the Marlins, I say, let's not, and say we did. Let's tax the tourists, but instead use the money to set up a fund designed to make the public school teachers of Miami-Dade County the best paid teachers in the country. Let's make sure that all of the talented, dedicated educators currently forming part of the system stay there. And let's make sure that those who have the talent and desire to teach, but haven't done so in the past because they could make so much more money elsewhere, follow their passion without having to sacrifice their bank accounts.

I'm sure a Diamond named Dontrelle would support such a proposal.

Update

As I write this update in May 2008, things seem to be once again on track for a retractable-roof baseball park to be built at the site of the legendary but now demolished Orange Bowl stadium. So Miami-Dade County, which, through flagrant neglect and mismanagement allowed the historic, memory-filled Orange Bowl to gradually degenerate into a pathetic, creaky hulk beyond repair, will now be entrusted to use our tax dollars *(continues)* to build and maintain a new ballpark. I guess they didn't think much of my proposal! Meanwhile, Dontrelle Willis, along with star third baseman Miguel Cabrera, was traded to the Detroit Tigers during the off-season since the Marlins, whose average attendance is about 5,000, cannot afford to pay them what they are worth in the open market.

No, Virginia

February 3, 2006

"VIRGINIA, YOUR LITTLE friends are wrong . . . Yes Virginia, there is a Santa Claus!"

So exclaimed the New York Sun in its reply to a little girl who, in 1897, intrepidly questioned the existence of everyone's favorite corpulent gift deliverer. The Sun's response to Virginia was universally applauded at the time, since it famously reassured the eight-year-old, and somehow accomplished this without actually lying. (Please see http://en.wikisource.org/wiki/Yes%2C_Virginia%2C_there_is_a_Santa_Claus for the full text of Virginia O'Hanlon's letter and the Sun's response, written by Francis Pharcellus Church.)

Yet the Sun's response, if examined clinically, is no more than a tongue-in-cheek, patronizing collection of half-truths, designed to mislead poor Virginia into continuing to earnestly believe what she has been told for years, even though it is a complete fabrication. It's like the entire adult population of the world is conspiring to defraud Virginia, and even a world-renowned newspaper, damn it, is in on the conspiracy!

Sort of reminds me of the outstanding 1998 film *The Truman Show*, in which Jim Carrey convincingly played Truman Burbank, a man whose entire life was covered live by television, worldwide, and everyone in the world knew that the people in Truman's life were all actors, and his entire world was a sound stage. Everyone knew, of course, except for the "star" of the 24-hour-a-day, 7-day-a-week show, the hapless Mr. Burbank.

Now I'm sure that if you actually saw The Truman Show, you were outraged by those who exploited Truman's whole life for the sake of ratings and product placement dollars. And you felt empathy for poor Truman, ostensibly loved by a global audience, but in reality made a fool of during every second of his pathetic, contrived life. Yet it is accepted practice to lie to children about Santa Claus, the Tooth Fairy, the Bogeyman . . . all sorts of things, and perpetuate the lies until the child grows old enough to figure out she's been duped. To what end, I ask? Why? I've heard various explanations, most of which boil down to something like, "Let's let him be a child as long as he can," or "What's wrong with giving her something magical to believe in?"

Now, far be it from your Sifter Stickers staff to judge or criticize anyone's child-rearing practices. However, we at Sifter Stickers abhor the practice of lying to our children, and we will make our case forthwith, first on a purely practical level, then from a more philosophical standpoint.

From an entirely pragmatic perspective, we ask, how can children reconcile what they are constantly learning about the way in which the world around them works with supposed facts—coming at them from their most trusted authority figures, no less—that completely contradict the rules they are attempting to internalize? "Yes, Virginia, gravity is an immutable law of nature, but there's an exception made for certain reindeer and overweight men once a year." A bit confusing, perhaps? "Don't worry, Virginia, our home is safe, except for that chimney, through which anyone can simply stroll in. Oh, and also, a strange creature will enter your room sometime tonight, while you're asleep, and take your tooth away and leave money in its place." Not exactly reassuring!

But by far the worst aspect of the lies is that they will, inexorably, catch up to you. And you can count on this, dear reader: the pain brought by the inevitable eventual shattering of these beliefs more than negates the pleasure they supposedly brought during their short-lived inclusion in the child's set of universal truths. Different kids learn about reality at different times, and those who learn first are seldom considerate or gentle when they break the news to their innocent, still-believing classmates! And, probably worst of all, how does a parent appropriately respond to a child who cannot fathom how her parents lied to her for all of these years? There simply is no valid response, because the action itself is not defensible. And it will take time and effort to regain your child's trust.

On the philosophical side, obviously parents' intentions when lying to their children are noble. Parents understandably want to bring as much happiness and excitement into their children's lives as they possibly can, and Santa, the Tooth Fairy, and others of their ilk represent easy ways of attaining those noble goals—at least in the short term. But in reality, it's rather sad to have to resort to fantasy to bring happiness to children, particularly since they would probably be happier with the truth.

You don't believe me? OK, pretend you're five years old. Which of the following scenarios would make you feel happier (of course, being about Santa Claus, the stories assume you are of the Christian faith):

1. Father says: "OK, it's Christmas, so we are celebrating the birth of an amazing man who we believe is actually God. So, there's this overweight man who lives in the North Pole, see, and he magically knows how well you've behaved all year. He also knows what you would like to get for Christmas, because he got your letter, so he will fly on a sleigh pulled by magic reindeer to every house in the world, and deliver toys to every child. You'll get yours,

like everyone else, and they'll be under the Christmas tree tomorrow morning when you wake up, so we'll all get together and open them."

2. Father says: "OK, it's Christmas, so we are celebrating the birth of an amazing man who we believe is actually God. So, your mom and I love you very much, and since you've been such a good boy this year, to celebrate Christmas we'll get you some really cool presents, ones that we know you want (see, we've been paying attention to you all year), and place them under the Christmas tree, and when you wake up tomorrow morning we'll all get together and open them."

OK, which one would you rather hear? I rest my case. Now, about this God thing . . .

Freedom

February 11, 2006

LITTLE DID I realize it at the time, but August 1995 marked the beginning of a momentous shift in my work life: the slow but steady metamorphosis from an office-bound paradigm to, eventually, the freedom (or the slavery—we'll get into that!) of a backpack-based workflow.

Sometime during that fateful month (the exact date is, alas, long forgotten) I received my shiny new Toshiba Satellite notebook, my first-ever portable computer. The little Satellite packed a potent punch for the time: an Intel 80486 processor, 12MB of RAM, and a then huge 500MB hard drive, all run by the ubiquitous Windows 3.1. (In 1995 I was totally engulfed by the DOS/Windows darkness. I would finally see the Macintosh light six years later.) But most importantly, the Toshiba obliterated my previous computers' chains to the desktop, and ushered me into the world of portable computing, a world which I still, over ten years later, cheerfully inhabit.

Around the time I was beginning to understand the implications of a computer that I could actually pick up and take with me, Motorola was transitioning from the now-hilarious looking

DynaTac "mobile" phone to the sleek, amazingly enduring clamshell design of the StarTac. Now, you could lug the DynaTac around, even though when you used it you looked like you were absurdly talking into a brick. And yes, both Apple and Compaq had released "portable" computers in the mid-to-late '80s, but just the thought of actually carrying one of those beasts with you while out and about was enough to generate deep back pain. (Just for the record, the 1989 Macintosh "luggable" weighed in at 15.8 pounds, while the Compaq "Doan's" Portable, introduced 7 years earlier in 1982, tipped the scales at a whopping 28 pounds!) So, at least to me, 1995, and the arrival of my Toshiba Satellite clearly marked the beginning of the mobile workplace.

Before my 1995 Toshiba, when I left my office, there was not much I could do work-wise. Yes, I could make phone calls from home, or even on the outrageously expensive DynaTac, but even then, I was computer-centric enough to want to use the ol' desktop for anything of substance. And no one else was working anyway. So quitting time was well defined. You left the office, and called it a day.

Fast forward ten years.

For years now, the requirements of my work have made it impossible for me to have a traditional office, in the sense of a place where I spend most of my work time and keep most of my work things. Instead, I have my backpack. And as long as I can have a reasonably fast Internet connection, I can do just about anything I need to using my PowerBook, my cell phone, and a few other accessories I carry on my back every day. I do keep an office, and deeply appreciate the times that I am able to enjoy it as a quiet sanctuary, but these days its main function is to house our servers, and allow them the bandwidth they need to, well, serve.

Thing is, at almost any given time all I need to do everything I need to do is at my fingertips. If I'm home, my PowerBook (along with a few other Macs) is on and at the ready, with the Internet available wirelessly everywhere. On the road, there's always a Starbucks, Barnes & Noble, or even

McDonald's nearby. Failing that, my Treo can serve as a rudimentary email checker or even Web browser. When traveling, even on "vacation," Internet access is ubiquitous, cell phone service is almost universal, and the backpack rarely leaves my side.

So, the question becomes, dear reader, when is "leisure" time? Or, maybe more precisely, what is leisure time?

No longer defined by technical capability or geography, leisure time becomes purely a state of mind. And, since my PowerBook is not only an astoundingly powerful work tool but a gateway to all sorts of recreational activities as well, the line is blurred even further. The "leisure" state of mind one might be enjoying while, say, browsing through new music at the iTunes Store, catching up on some reading, or enjoying some family photos, can be irrevocably altered by a single click on that hugely tempting email Dock icon, or on a browser bookmark to a router configuration page. Or a click on TextEdit to start a new Sifter Stickers essay . . . but wait a minute, is that work, or is it "leisure"? Which prompts me to ask again, does the difference lie? If you enjoy what you do for a living, is it still "work"?

In vintage Sifter Stickers fashion, we leave the tough questions thoroughly unanswered. But one thing we can say is that the backpack workflow allows unprecedented flexibility. The line between work and leisure is faint, and easily crossed at any time. Never have we had such power. And, if we are to keep our priorities where we ultimately want them to be, we must remember Spider-Man's credo: "With great power comes great responsibility."

Obtrusive

February 14, 2006

IT HAS BEEN said, and enthusiastically agreed to on these pages, that the beauty of Mac OS X is that it "gets out of the way" and enables you to do what you set out to do, without making its presence felt unless you call upon it. This is opposed to other operating systems of perhaps higher market presence, which are, along with their necessary supplementary programs, constantly, uncomfortably, in your face.

And the fact that Mac OS X is unobtrusive makes it an even more pleasurable experience to explore it and discover its inner beauty, perhaps even delve deep into the operating system's Unix core. Mac OS X does not shout; it elegantly beckons. Mac OS X respects our space.

And as we ponder the nuances that differentiate operating systems and, really, software in general, it becomes obvious that what applies to our computer also applies to the people around us!

The people with whom we enjoy spending time are those who, like Mac OS X, respect our space. People with whom we can share a thoughtful silence. People who will suggest when appropriate, but whose strong support is not predicated on whether or not we follow their suggestions. People who are not in our face.

People sensitive enough to understand what our fundamental objectives are, and transparent enough to help us attain those objectives without thought to their own agenda.

I would venture to say that the proportion of obtrusive to unobtrusive people on the planet is similar to the proportion of Windows computers to Macs. Which makes it common for all of us to constantly deal with the obtrusive ones, the "space invaders," if we may liken them to those odious, relentlessly advancing aliens of the legendary video game.

And which also makes it all the more remarkable for us to spend time with those who, like Mac OS X, elegantly beckon, irresistibly drawing us to explore the beauty within.

Let the Music Take You
February 28, 2006

WHEN YOU MENTION the Carpenters, most people think of a sappy duo from the '70s whose music is best limited to elevators. To me, though, the gorgeous voice of Karen Carpenter is an immediate ticket to Sunday afternoon "dancing parties" circa 1972. At those events, Ms. Carpenter's rich vocalizations meant only one thing to us boys: quick action would enable us to hold that special girl impossibly close, and experience the delicious butterflies that magically sprouted from our awakening hormones and fluttered all over our stomachs, not to mention other unmentionable places.

Other music of the era affects me in similar ways: Roberta Flack's "Killing Me Softly With His Song" also hastily brings to heart those early slow dances of self discovery. Any cut from Peter Frampton's *Frampton Comes Alive* album immediately transports me to other, perhaps more mundane, events of my youth, as do songs from one-hit wonders like Deep Purple ("Smoke on the Water," of course) and Golden Earring (who could forget "Radar Love"?). Yet the music most often played by oldies and "classic rock" radio stations does not have that effect:

Led Zeppelin's "Stairway to Heaven," for example, takes me absolutely nowhere, as does the Aerosmith classic "Dream On." And while I enjoy music by Elton John, Billy Joel, and The Eagles, most of it has also somehow lost its ability to transcend time and space.

Which brings me to today's Sifter Sticker: the realization that, ironically, every time you listen to a song from the past, you drain away a little bit of its power to transport you there. Karen Carpenter means the beginning of adolescent intimacy to me simply because I have hardly listened to her voice during the intervening 33 years. Billy Joel's "Piano Man," also released in the early '70s, no longer has the power to evoke a specific memory because, let's face it, I've probably listened to it hundreds of times while sitting in traffic on I-95.

This, dear reader, is the epitome of sweet sorrow. The notes of a long-forgotten tune provide you with a lightning-fast conduit to a sweet memory. Yet as you listen, and savor, you realize that the conduit is that much weaker, and will continue to weaken if, by happenstance or design, you have the opportunity to savor it again. So, in the age of the iPod, where any song you have ever heard can be yours to listen to at your convenience, you must weigh the joy of the experience against its own gradual, yet inevitable, erosion. Because (staying with the early '70s theme), like one of Jim Phelps' tapes ("your mission, should you choose to accept it . . .") the feeling is relentlessly self-destructive.

We're All in Stockholm

March 8, 2006

I TRAVEL QUITE frequently, and despite the ever-increasing hassles that go along with today's air travel, find it to be a generally pleasurable experience. The actual time on the airplane itself often provides a welcome opportunity to catch up on reading, or to tackle offline tasks that require relatively long, uninterrupted stretches of time, which are increasingly scarce in my everyday life.

Although I've been fortunate enough not to have been involved in any air-travel-related emergencies so far, I have, of course, experienced my fair share of heavy turbulence, minor mechanical malfunctions, and other mildly unpleasant incidents. Invariably, these incidents are followed by relieved travelers humbly thanking their deity of choice for enabling them to escape the perilous situation unscathed.

I've always found a fascinating incongruence in these utterances. We are faced with a situation that scares us. Once the scary part is over, our first impulse is to thank a purportedly all-powerful entity for saving us from harm. And apparently our overwhelming relief at being spared further unpleasantness (or much worse) serves to blind us to that shy student with the raised hand in the back of our brain's classroom, the one who would sheepishly remind us that logic dictates that if the all-powerful entity had the power, will, and moment of spare time to save us from impending doom, it could have prevented us from experiencing the scary situation to begin with!

We've all heard someone say something like, "Hey, I was in an accident today, my car is totaled, I broke my arm, but, thank God, I'm OK." Cool, but wouldn't it be just as valid for the same person, after the same incident, to say, "Hey, I was in an accident today, curse the Lord, and broke my arm and totaled my car!" No one seems to say that. Many people, when asked how they are doing, will always either preface or follow any positive response with "thank God." But how many people have you heard respond to the same question negatively, and express their displeasure with the entity that they obviously believe is responsible?

According to the relatively young yet already venerable Wikipedia, the Stockholm Syndrome is "a psychological response sometimes seen in a hostage, in which the hostage exhibits seeming loyalty to the hostage-taker, in spite of the danger (or at least risk) the hostage has been put in." Named after the "robbery of Kreditbanken at Norrmalmstorg, Stockholm in which the bank robbers held bank employees hostage from August 23 to August 28, 1973," the "Stockholm syndrome is also sometimes discussed in reference to other situations with similar tensions, such as battered woman syndrome and child abuse cases." Even more to the point, in its article about the Stockholm Syndrome and its offshoot "capture-bonding," Wikipedia further states that "Loyalty to a more powerful abuser . . . is common among victims of domestic abuse, battered partners and child abuse (dependent children)."

One could easily argue that anyone subjected to an uncontrollable situation perceived as being life threatening is in the same fragile state of mind as the women at the Kreditbanken. And, if the person believes in the existence of an all-powerful entity, then obviously this entity is the party in control, as were the bank robbers in Stockholm, and as were the Symbionese Liberation Army operatives in the similar Patty Hearst case of 1974. So it should be no surprise that, in apparent defiance of logic, the person will generally react with loyalty, or bonding, with the entity that placed her in danger to begin with, just as the Stockholm women and Ms. Hearst did. Just as a newborn baby forms "an emotional attachment to the nearest powerful adult in order to maximize the probability that this adult will enable—at the very least—the survival of the child . . ." (once again, Wikipedia), we tend to reach out to the most powerful force we perceive to be available to us in times of danger, even if we would admit (probably under some coercion, to be sure) that the same force is responsible for placing us in danger in the first place.

Loyalty toward a more powerful abuser. An undisputed human characteristic. As Gus Portokalos would sum up, "There you go."

Although the "thank God" reaction continues to defy logic, at least it seems to be consistent with other human behavior, as explained by the Stockholm Syndrome and its offshoot, "capture-bonding." And you could make the case that as we go about our danger filled lives, where pitfalls abound and disaster is always lurking nearby, we are continuously held hostage to our fears. So it's only natural for those who believe that their lives are under the strict control of an all-powerful entity to show loyalty toward the "more powerful abuser."

Windows on the Mac

March 24, 2006

SO, IT FINALLY happened. We all knew it would, ever since that fateful morning in June 2005, when Steve uttered, "It's true." The rumors were no longer rumors; they were fact. Future Macintosh computers would be powered by Intel processors. There would be a transition. There would be change.

And the change came fast. First the new iMacs, followed quickly by the lamentably named MacBook Pro, and, most recently, the Mac mini. All Intel-powered. As will be the entire Apple lineup by the end of the year.

And the transition is going well. No question, transparent emulation marvel Rosetta exceeded everyone's performance expectations. Native apps are screamers on the Intel machines, and developers are generating universal binaries at a healthy clip. The only ones momentarily left behind are the heavy Adobe CS2 and Apple Pro App users, but not for long. The transition will be complete by year's end, and from all indications it will have been an amazing accomplishment.

Yet, as much as it all smells sweet, the inevitable event of this week, the one that was set in motion that fine San Francisco morning last June, permeates the sweet smell with the subtle yet undeniable scent of decay. Because that which we knew would happen, albeit exciting on one level, is terrifying on another.

Yes, of course we refer to the successful installation of Windows XP on Mac hardware. As we all knew someone would, someone did find a way to get around the EFI/BIOS issues and boot Windows on a Mac. And everyone is excited. Isn't this great? John Q, who wants to use a Mac but doesn't because a couple of his critical applications are Windows only, can now buy a MacBook Pro, and just boot into Windows when needed! Apple will sell so many more Macs! Finally, Apple will make significant market share inroads!

But will this event forever be remembered as the beginning of the tragic, untimely end of our beloved Mac OS X?

Think about it. Once the driver and video issues are resolved, and Windows runs not only smoothly but really, really fast on Mac hardware, what possible incentive does a Windows developer have to develop Mac OS X versions of his software? Hey, Mac user, just boot into Windows! We don't need to port our software! Mac-only developers will find their products suddenly competing against Windows applications, as the nature of the "Mac space" changes dramatically.

Of course, traditional Windows PC buyers will flock to the Mac, since they will at last be able to enjoy Apple's unparalleled industrial design and hardware quality, while running their familiar operating system and software. Traditional Mac users will continue to run Mac OS X, of course, and everyone will know that it is the superior operating system. But will any developers be attracted to the Mac OS X platform if they can just develop Windows apps and cover both the traditional Windows PC space as well as the Mac (running Windows) market?

Does Windows on the Mac mean that Apple will sell a lot more computers, but Mac OS X will die? Was John C. Dvorak right? Will Windows become the Mac OS?

Well, Microsoft would benefit, as they would sell more copies of their flagship software. And Microsoft is, no doubt, a software company. And Apple would sell more computers, and Apple is, no doubt, a hardware company.

And we would use our beautiful machines, whose exterior would remind us of the glory we once had, but whose screens would sadly jar us back to our dreary new reality.

Maybe your Sifter Stickers staff is alarmist and overly pessimistic. We would like nothing more than to be dead wrong. In fact, we would love to look back on this column two years from now and laugh about its unfulfilled, bleak implications.

But amid all the excitement, we do not like this. We do not like this at all.

Update

If "dead wrong" was what I truly wanted to be, boy did I get my wish! Of course, Apple's transition to Intel processors brought with it the possibility of running Windows on Mac hardware, which has become legitimate and rather common. But I underestimated the power of Mac OS X, and overestimated the allure of Windows. The seamless running of Windows on the Mac did not adversely affect the development of applications for Mac OS X at all; in fact Mac OS X is thriving as never before. I guess I was alarmist and pessimistic about this, as I tend to be in general. But the good thing about being alarmist and pessimistic is that one is seldom disappointed!

Cynicism
March 22, 2006

IT'S EASY TO be cynical these days.

Seems like half of Congress is illicitly involved with lobbyists, and the other half self-righteously expounds on the other's failings—until it's their turn to get caught. Pharmaceutical companies convert everyday annoyances into medical conditions that can be controlled with drugs, which have such terrifying possible side effects that the requisite commercials laughably attempt to sweep the required warning voiceover under a carpet of sweet music and tranquil scenery. Greedy corporate leaders constantly find ways to bilk the government, their shareholders, the public at large, or all of the above.

You get the picture. Even though we haven't even mentioned unscrupulous stockbrokers preying on elderly retirees, opportunistic lawyers attempting to extract money from companies for serving hot coffee, or even the astonishing fact that the greed of our country's telecommunications and cable television companies, which control our access to the Internet, have kept our broadband speeds well below those in many Asian and European nations.

It is difficult to determine if there are more reasons to become cynical today than there were in the past, or if the increasing cynicism of your Sifter Stickers staff is simply a byproduct of its increasing, ahem, maturity. Our initial impulse is to stick with the former, since it is far easier to contemplate the decay of the world around us than to consider that what may be in decay happens to reside inside our skull . . . but then again, maturity does bring with it more than just organic deterioration. It brings experience, a trait impossible to teach or otherwise transmit to others. A trait that may only be acquired in the old-fashioned way John Houseman used to proclaim Smith Barney made its money: by earning it.

And experience seems to bring cynicism right along with it, like the sidecars attached to those comical motorcycles used by the hapless Germans on *Hogan's Heroes*. So the brash idealism and innocence of youth are gradually supplanted by weary worldliness. We are not surprised to hear that, say, former congressman "Duke" Cunningham collected over $2.4 million in bribes during his 15-year stint in the House of Representatives, or that former president Bill Clinton, whose wife, of course, is currently a U.S. senator, is an acknowledged paid lobbyist for the government of Dubai, United Arab Emirates. We read these items with a resigned shake of the head, and chalk it up to the myriad character deficiencies afflicting our species. Deficiencies which make it necessary for us to have umpires and referees, hall monitors and security guards, policemen and lawyers. Judges. Armies.

Stephen Falken, a character from the outstanding 1983 movie *War Games*, is the epitome of cynicism. At one point in the film, Falken, played by John Wood, shows the main characters (played by Mathew Broderick and Ally Sheedy) a film about dinosaurs, and explains how they once ruled the earth, and then suddenly disappeared. Nature, Falken somberly intoned, simply gave up and started over. The implication was that the same fate awaited our own species, and it was only a matter of time before nature gave up and started over once again. Of course, in true Hollywood fashion, Falken's cynicism was no match for the younger characters' (shall we quote the great Alan Greenspan) "irrational exuberance," and so the destruction of our species was, momentarily, at least, averted.

Does reality reflect the cinematically attractive notion that the goodness in all of us will ultimately triumph over our failings? Or is it only a matter of time before nature needs to "start over"? Will we bring the destruction of our species upon ourselves, or will we hang on long enough to be destroyed by a comet striking our planet, or some other catastrophic event beyond our control? Or, will we be the species that transcends time and space, and becomes one with the universe?

Tantalizing questions, no doubt. But I'm sure that if the bookmakers at Las Vegas, a cynical lot indeed, were laying odds, the self-destruction of the human race would be the overwhelming favorite—and its enlightenment a monumental longshot.

Update

There seem to be more reasons than ever to be cynical. Hilary Clinton, in 2006 a U.S. Senator whose former president husband was a paid lobbyist for a foreign government, was later, of course, a contender for the presidency herself. And while "Duke" Cunningham faded into the sunset in 2006, many other members of congress have since joined the ranks of the corrupt. Humanity's eventual enlightenment seems like even more of a long shot, while it's eventual self-destruction feels like a foregone conclusion.

The Light Turns Red

April 5, 2006

THE LIGHT TURNS red. And the boy (eight years old, perhaps nine) races from one stopped car to another, delicately placing a box of candy at the base of the driver's side window of each one. He balances the box just right so that it stays put. He tries to time it so that he maximizes the number of candy boxes showcased, but still allows enough time to pick up those boxes simply ignored by the drivers (usually all of them) and maybe, just maybe, complete the sale of a box or two before the light turns green. A brief rest. The light turns red again.

And yes, once in a while some jerk will open his window, take the candy, and refuse to pay. Yet the boy has found that the showcase method is more effective than the traditional car-to-car offering method he employed in the past, even allowing for the occasional shoplifter. Marketing 101 on the streets of Bogota. The professor is hunger. The boy learns fast. The light turns red again.

The boy is filthy, but the grime can't cover the intelligence in his eyes. The interminable monotony can't defeat the boy's enthusiasm. The squalor can't sully the boy's integrity. The futility of it all can't dampen the hope.

Most drivers simply ignore the boy and his candy. Why not, there are thousands like him, and in a short, five-mile drive through Bogota you are likely to have candy showcased on your car window at least four or five times. You are also likely to see other enterprising boys juggle flaming batons during traffic stops, or perform a mime show. All for the remote possibility that a couple of jaded drivers will find the shows worthy of spare change.

The boy gingerly places the candy box on the car window, and quickly darts to the next car in line. The man in the car gets a quick look at the boy, and thinks of what might have been. Thinks of his son, roughly the same age. Same set of intelligent brown eyes, impossibly different set of opportunities. The boy comes back and favors the man with a hopeful glance. The man opens his window, hands the boy money, tells him to keep the candy, too. They exchange a smile. The light turns green.

That night the man wonders what the boy is doing. If he is warm, on this cold Andean night. If he is still at it, eagerly placing candy boxes on car windows, giving the drivers a hopeful glance before removing the box a few seconds later. Where will he sleep? What will he eat?

Throughout the city, thousands of lights turn red.

Nuggets

April 17, 2006

THIS WEEK'S ESSAY offers a sampling of Sifter Sticker Nuggets, or items perhaps interesting enough for momentary reflection (and maybe a thoughtful "hmmm"), but clearly not worthy of further research or development in their own right. A Sifter Sticker miscellanies, if you will, of random, unrelated thoughts, in no particular order:

1. Christian is a fairly common name. So, why isn't anyone out there named Jew or Muslim?
2. If it is spelled Favre (Packer quarterback Brett), why is it pronounced Farve?
3. Why do we say "stop by" when we mean "come to"? For example, "stop by the house this afternoon"? Does this mean we are to stop just short of the house and wait there?
4. Why do men have nipples?
5. Why is fecal matter known as "stool"?
6. On that topic, why is "shit" considered to be a "bad word"? And "rape" not? Still on that topic, who decided which words are "bad"? Which country was the first to begin

driving on the "other" side of the road (whatever side that was), and why? Why is it called "common sense," since it clearly is not?
7. Besides to create confusion, why do most Romance languages assign a gender to inanimate objects?
8. Why is the Unit Production Manager usually the first person listed in movie credits?
9. Cats, unlike dogs, are concerned enough about their hygiene to clean themselves up subsequent to bowel movements. And they do this with their tongue! I would not have believed this, except I recently saw it with my own eyes. Talk about a Sifter Sticker! More than stuck, the image seems to have permanently bonded to my mind.

Update

Brett Favre is now a New York Jet. The bizarre pronunciation of his surname continues unabated.

Immigration

April 17, 2006

AS THE DEBATE rages on between advocates of a "get tough" immigration policy and those who favor amnesty for illegal aliens, it seems to me that what we have is actually an amazing opportunity, well disguised as a crisis.

Think of it. We live in a nation that millions of people in other parts of the world risk life and limb to sneak into, in order to have the economic opportunities and political freedom that we take for granted. People want to come here, and in the vast majority of cases are simply looking for a better life for their families, fully willing to work long and hard to attain it.

Our current immigration policy seems hopelessly confused between the ideals so indelibly symbolized by our Statue of Liberty ("Give me your poor . . . ") and the closed-minded, childlike paranoia of those who fear that our nation will be overrun by welfare-abusing criminals. So, we grant Cubans automatic refugee status if they are able to somehow make it to our shores, but we do our level best to stop them before they make it. To would-be immigrants from Mexico, or Colombia, or virtually anywhere else in Latin America, we say sorry, we're closed, and even if they do somehow get in, they are subject to immediate deportation. The so-called justification for this duality is, of course, that Cuba is a communist country, and we give refuge to the politically persecuted—but not to the merely economically challenged.

The widely held justification for maintaining our closed borders is that immigrants will take "American" jobs, promoting unemployment for U.S. citizens. So, we continue to outsource manufacturing, call centers, and technical support to companies based in foreign countries due to their cheaper labor costs, while we refuse entry to people totally willing to work for wages similar to those prevalent in many of those same foreign countries. We continue to hire illegal immigrants to do those jobs deemed undesirable by everyone else, paying them wages well below legal minimums. We endorse the status quo when it benefits us, and rally against it when it does not.

The argument that allowing people within our borders to work for lower wages will divide our society and create a class of people with substandard income rings hollow to anyone who has spent time in East L.A., Liberty City in Miami, or in the similar areas that exist in every major American city. Let's face it: our country is already divided, and those on the south side of the divide are not only illegal immigrants already working for sublegal wages—there are plenty of bona fide U.S. citizens there as well.

Obviously this is a complex issue, and I do not pretend to have anywhere near all the answers. What I do have is a fresh perspective: let's liken the immigration situation to every other situation where we have tried to make people act in ways contrary to their primary motivations. Prohibition. Celibacy for priests. The "war" on drugs. None of them works, and instead, unsurprisingly, they spawn undesirable behaviors. Everyone loses.

Instead of knee-jerk reactions resulting in an expensive, uphill battle with no possible victory, let's carefully consider the situation. We have millions of prospective model citizens at our gates who are willing to work hard and become productive members of our society. We have millions of people already inside, who are already working hard to support their families, but due to their illegal status are not contributing into the system at all, representing significant resource leakage. We need to come up with ways of harnessing these awesome resources, ways that prove favorable to all parties. This is clearly not a zero-sum, mutually exclusive situation; it is an unprecedented opportunity for out-of-the-box thinking.

As difficult as it is to deal with millions of people at our door, let's not forget the alternative: a sad, empty space where those people used to be, because our country is no longer the place the world looks to for opportunity.

Diversity

April 30, 2006

For more than 50 years, Bing Crosby's rendition of "White Christmas" was recognized as the best-selling single in any musical category. It was played so often in the years following its initial release in 1942 that the master tape was actually damaged due to frequent use, and in March 1947, Crosby, the Trotter Orchestra, and the Darby Singers, all of whom collaborated in the original recording, were called back to Decca Records' studios to re-record the song. Few people would dispute that "White Christmas" figures prominently in the definitive list of Americana. And speaking of things American, with the exception of "The Star Spangled Banner," no song is more frequently chosen to express patriotism than "God Bless America," widely considered the United States' "unofficial" national anthem. Both "White Christmas" and "God Bless America" were written by American composer and lyricist Irving Berlin (1888–1989), who wrote over 3,000 songs, many of them hugely popular hits on Broadway and Hollywood. No doubt, Berlin left an indelible mark on American music and culture.

Few movies are as familiar to Americans as Frank Capra's *It's a Wonderful Life*. The classic "feel good" story leaves few dry eyes in the audience whenever it is shown, despite the fact that everyone has seen it at least 47 times. In addition to *It's a Wonderful Life*, American Director Capra (1897–1991) was also responsible for classics such as the Oscar-winning romantic comedy *It Happened One Night*, *Mr. Deeds Goes to Town*, *Lost Horizon* and *Mr. Smith Goes to Washington*, among many others.

No person has become as synonymous with a noun as American scientist Albert Einstein has with the word "genius." Widely regarded as the most important scientist of the 20th century, he is the author of the special and general theories of relativity and made significant contributions to quantum mechanics, statistical mechanics, and cosmology. Albert Einstein (1879–1955) is quite possibly the most famous scientist in history, and was chosen by *Time* magazine as the Person of the Century on December 31, 1999.

As you ponder what our country would be like without Berlin's, Capra's and Einstein's contributions, consider this: each of them was an American by choice, not by accident of birth. Irving Berlin was born Israel Isidore Berlin in Tyumen, Russia. Frank Capra was born Francesco Rosario Capra in Bisacquino, Sicily, Italy. Albert Einstein was born in Ulm, Germany.

Other famous Americans that you may be surprised to learn were born elsewhere include Intel founder Andy Grove (Hungary), former Secretaries of State Henry Kissinger (Germany) and Madeline Albright (Czechoslovakia, now Czech Republic), violet-eyed actress Elizabeth Taylor (England), rocker Eddie Van Halen (Netherlands), talkie pioneer Al Jolson (Lithuania), 97-pound weakling converter Charles Atlas (Italy) and late American institution Bob Hope (England). In reality, though, unless you are a Native American, your family immigrated to the U.S. at some point in time. Therefore, someone in your family tree is an immigrant. The only question is how recent.

As we deal with the challenges brought on by our more contemporary immigration issues, let's not forget that our diversity is our strength. And that the next Albert Einstein may be suffocating in a sweltering truck in south central Texas. Or that the next Intel will not be founded if the next Andy Grove is turned back at the gate.

Focusing on "celebrity" immigrants is fun, and may be illustrative. However, the true impact of immigration on this country is vast to the point of being immeasurable, and is much more a product of the millions of immigrants we've never heard of than the hundreds we do know something about.

That said, I must leave you with this one: Chaim Witz was born in Israel on August 25, 1949. You know him as Gene Simmons, the blood-spurting, fire breathing, bass-playing rocker with 70's teen favorite band Kiss. Go figure.

More information: http://www.ailf.org/notable/famous.htm

Nuggets II

May 8, 2006

A S DID "NUGGETS" (page 99), the present essay offers another potpourri of bite-sized Sifter Stickers.

1. Signs on commercial airline bathrooms state (and I quote), "Discarding anything other than toilet tissue in the toilet can cause external leaks and create a safety hazard." This warning clearly implies that that we should place our human liquid and solid waste products somewhere other than the toilet! Like where, the sink perhaps?

    Other signs, a bit more specific, read (once again, I quote), "Please use the trash container for anything other than toilet tissue." A pretty nasty idea, if you ask me.

2. Speaking of air travel, why do people, depending on their religious persuasion, cross themselves, or say the Shema (affirmation of Judaism and a declaration of faith in one God), or pray in one way or another during takeoff? Assuming you are a staunch believer in God (which would seem to be a prerequisite for the act itself), don't you be-

lieve that God is always with you? Does he need reminding that hey, you are about to take part in a hazardous activity (for the moment, let's ignore the fact that air travel is less hazardous than, say, taking a shower) and he needs to be particularly sharp in order to protect you? Does it mean that the lives of all others on the airplane with you are worth nothing, and God would usually allow them to perish, but since you are on board and have asked for "special" help, then God will make sure that your particular flight is safe? Is God the type of entity that would allow hundreds of people to die simply because you failed to affirm your belief in him before becoming airborne?
3. Are gay people aroused by their own bodies? (Not that there's anything wrong with that!)
4. Speaking of arousal, why are men aroused by lesbian porn (I've heard), yet women not aroused by gay male porn (at least according to the handful of women I've had the audacity to ask)?
5. Consider the traditional greeting, "How do you do?" Exactly what does that mean? How do you do what?
6. Was it really chivalry, or did the guy who first held a door open for a woman just want to get a good look at her ass?

Land of . . .

May 15, 2006

I SPENT THE summer of 1972 at Camp Lenni-Len-A-Pe, in Salisbury Mills, New York. Given that most of my fellow campers lived in the surrounding upstate New York area, being from Colombia I was a bit of a novelty. But most of my 11-year-old bunkmates knew of Colombia, since it was the place where Juan Valdez was from—you know, the guy with the burro who picked the coffee beans. Some of the older campers associated my country of birth with a mysterious substance known as "Colombian Gold," but I had no idea what they were referring to. In later years, of course, I did find out what Colombian Gold was, and was proud, in a backhanded sort of way, that my native land produced what was considered the best quality marijuana in the world. A dubious claim to fame, to be sure, but at least my country was best at something.

So, in the 1970s, to most Americans, Colombia was the land of coffee and the land of pot.

During the 1980's, television detectives Sonny Crockett and Ricardo Tubbs stylishly battled Colombian cocaine lords (among other lowlife) in the streets and waterways of South Florida, as their series, *Miami Vice*, took the country by storm and helped put its namesake city back into America's consciousness. And while the pastel-clad, permanently coifed Crockett and Tubbs cavorted around gorgeous Miami on the small screen, moviegoers got to see Al Pacino's unforgettable Tony Montana claw his way to the top of the drug lord heap (in Miami, of course), despite the chain-saw wielding Colombian gangs in his way. In the eyes of America my country had been transformed from the tranquil home of serene coffee pickers and weed growers to the vile lair of violently deranged cocaine cowboys who would hack off your arm in a bathtub if crossed.

During the '90s Colombia's struggle with local guerilla movements came to the forefront, as the drug lords and insurgents formed a powerful alliance. Violence escalated, as did Colombia's disrepute in the U.S. Most Americans perceived Colombia as a lawless, frighteningly violent place, and movies like *Clear and Present Danger* and *Proof of Life* supported the view.

I lived in Colombia for most of the first seventeen years of my life, and although I've lived in the United States since 1978, I've also spent plenty of time In Colombia since then, either on business or visiting family. And yes, there is some veracity in the picture of Colombia that most Americans have historically had in their minds. But the truth is that, although Colombia is many things, it is, more than anything else, a land of intelligent, resourceful, hardworking people, and a land of spectacular beauty.

Speaking of beauty, we finally arrive at this week's Sifter Sticker. This weekend, a gentleman from Florida Power & Light who was performing an energy survey on my home asked me where I was born. When I said Colombia, unlike my Bunk 6 colleagues from Lenni-Len-A-Pe he did not think of coffee or Juan Valdez. He did not think of pot, either. The mention of Colombia did not conjure up images of drug dealers with chain saws, or guerrillas with machine guns.

Instead, he indicated that his niece had recently visited Colombia for the surgical enhancement of her breasts. He also mentioned that many of her colleagues at the law firm where she works had done the same. All were satisfied with the results, as well as with the overall experience. Seems like, previously unbeknownst to me, Colombia has become a Mecca for those seeking medical attention of a, shall we say, elective nature. High quality, reasonable costs, you see.

My U.S. passport clearly states, on page 1, that I was born in Colombia. I'm as proud of the passport as I am of the birthplace. So it gave me great pleasure to hear that my native land has become a place Americans want to go to, instead of stay away from. And so I say to those who travel to Colombia for a bit more here, or a bit less there: look around. You'll like what you see. Colombia will perk up your heart, as well as your breasts!

Thank You, God

May 22, 2006

As Barry Bonds finally arrives at home plate after casually trotting around the bases upon hitting a home run, he unfailingly brings his fingers to his mouth, kisses them, and opens up his hands while projecting them skyward, ending up in a pose reminiscent of an NFL referee signaling a touchdown. Except that, while NFL referees usually look straight ahead while making their most dramatic of signals, Mr. Bonds theatrically looks toward the heavens, in an apparently humble gesture of thanks.

Now, "humble" is a word seldom seen in a sentence about Barry Bonds, except when used in a sarcastic sense. Yet the reputedly arrogant Mr. Bonds seems to be attributing at least some of the credit for his feat to a higher power. But although the left fielder's gesture may superficially seem deferential, further analysis rapidly dispels that notion.

Think about it, dear reader: Bonds is implying that God has astonishingly chosen to ignore the pleas of starving children, while assisting him in his quest for a 23rd luxury automobile. The entity upstairs has somehow deemed Mr. Bonds's need for more jewelry more deserving of his attention than the life of the innocent victim of a stray bullet a few miles away from the ballpark.

Many of us have much to be thankful for. I, for one, consider myself fortunate to the extreme. And when we feel fortunate it seems appropriate to somehow express appreciation for our privileges, lest we take our good fortune for granted. It seems the proper, humble thing to do.

Except it just doesn't make any sense.

Because if you thank God for your own good fortune you necessarily assume that God is a micro-manager in complete control of the minutiae of the universe, and cares more about you than about those who are not as fortunate as you are. Barry Bonds thanks God for his home run. But what about the pitcher who served up the gopher ball? Is he not as worthy of divine intervention as the allegedly steroid-enhanced specimen on his way around the bases? If you thank God for putting food on your table, you necessarily imply that he is responsible for putting it there. Doesn't that mean that he is then responsible for denying food from those who go to bed hungry? On what basis does he decide who eats and who doesn't?

Thanking God for good things puts him on the hook for bad things. And it seems there are a lot more bad things happening on our planet than good things.

It's enough to drive you directly into the welcoming arms of atheism.

The Hard Way

May 28, 2006

I RECENTLY READ that artificial sweeteners actually cause unsuspecting dieters to gain weight. This unfortunate result is the consequence of the body's sensing the sweet taste and expecting the requisite calories to go with it. When the calories inexplicably fail to materialize, the body absolutely craves them and seeks them elsewhere, leading the would-be dieter on the merry road to perdition. And even if our example dieter resists the immediate temptation, his constant use of artificial sweeteners accustoms his body to sweet-tasting substances, making it even more difficult than it would otherwise be to stick to healthy, non-sweet foods.

But the whole artificial sweetener craze (and it is a craze—the *Wall Street Journal* recently reported that Diet Pepsi will soon become Pepsi's flagship brand, displacing Pepsi itself!) points to a larger issue—so large, in fact, that it could eventually cause the human race's downfall . . . if we're lucky enough to make it that far. The issue is that we humans will eschew the simple, fundamental solution to a problem if it involves even a minor short-term sacrifice, as long as there is a solution available which is perceived to be painless, even if it is circuitous, superficial and myopic. We take the path of least resistance. We take the easy way out.

We want to cut out sugar from our diets because it is poison. But may the gods forbid that we forgo the sweet taste! So we simply switch from Coke to Diet Coke instead of to water. We cut out one poison, but our inability to adjust our taste makes us replace it with another poison! We take the easy way out, and therefore do not solve the root of the problem.

When fat was deemed to be the Great Threat to Humanity a few years back, all sorts of low-fat versions of fatty foods materialized. Hey, just because we shouldn't consume fat doesn't mean that we should deprive ourselves of the delicious experience of consuming fatty foods! Myriad products, representing billions of dollars in annual sales, were spawned solely to falsely placate our ill-advised desires.

Artificial sweeteners. Traditionally fatty foods with "lowered" fat. Appetite suppressants. Frivolous cosmetic surgeries. Gambling casinos, pyramid schemes. Decaffeinated coffee, alcohol-free beer. The lottery.

Forget about "no pain, no gain." We want gain, with absolutely no pain.

Trouble is, the pain is what makes the gain worthwhile. And if the gain comes without any pain, it just doesn't feel the same.

The point is that, in almost every case, the sweet anticipation of a perceived prize is as pleasurable as, and many times much more pleasurable than, the prize itself. And, relatedly, nothing in life, material or otherwise, may be properly appreciated without the benefit of comparison with the lack thereof.

Will we ever learn that the easy way is not necessarily the best way? That the process is, in most cases, far more rewarding than the result? That the reward for losing weight through adjustments to diet and lifestyle far transcends the weight loss itself? That a dollar won cannot compare to dollar earned?

Perhaps, but it sure doesn't seem that way from here.

Baseball and the News

June 4, 2006

TO ME, THE best way to watch a baseball game is not to watch it at all. Good radio baseball announcers do an amazing job of crafting an entire experience exclusively with words, so that listening to the game is actually better than being there. Not only does the announcer's word picture immerse me in the game, but there is that special warmth that comes from chatting with a friend, a feeling best exemplified by the legendary Vin Scully's immortal words, "pull up a chair and stick around awhile . . . ." You are sitting around a kitchen table, where a good friend, who happens to be perceptive and articulate, is gently telling you a story.

Baseball announcers are typically obsessed with accuracy in the details, and make a point of providing a pitch-by-pitch, absolutely precise rendition of the game, while using their considerable descriptive prowess to frame it within the atmosphere of the ballpark. Radio baseball announcers are fanatical about the integrity of their broadcasts, and if you happen to listen to a game while at the ballpark, you will quickly understand how good they are at capturing the experience and sending it off, unaltered, over the air.

Yet, if you've ever witnessed or been a part of any event "covered" by your local television news, you know that what you saw or experienced in person, and what was conveyed in the newscast, were two completely different things. Accuracy takes a back seat to hype. Integrity matters only if it can hold the audience for a few more minutes. Stories deemed tantalizing are shamelessly and incessantly "teased" prior to their actual airing, to a degree that the story itself is a hollow disappointment, typically providing very little information not already provided in the "tease" phase.

The same seems to happen with most print media coverage of events. Although there are, of course, many exceptions, in general, news media will describe events in a way that makes them seem more exciting than they actually were, or more relevant to more people, or skewed in a way to fit in with an internal, or hidden agenda. Sensationalism is commonplace; objectivity and accuracy are rare.

The hyperbole associated with news stories and their "spin" have become so commonplace that the genuineness of a baseball radio broadcast seems a throwback. An anomaly whose days, perhaps, are numbered. In the meantime, though, if you want to get away from breathless promotion, hype, hidden agendas and tired political rants, you may want to take Vin's gentle suggestion, and "pull up a chair." A warm chat around a kitchen table is a wonderful experience anytime.

So Many Pieces

June 11, 2006

THE LAST HOLIDAY is a well-executed tearjerker of a chick flick, in which the incomparable Queen Latifah plays Georgia Byrd, a kind, decent working woman from New Orleans who suddenly learns that she is afflicted with a rare disease, and will die within three weeks. Now I have no problem with so-called chick flicks; to me they simply represent another movie genre to be enjoyed. And I do have a soft spot in my heart for the Queen. So I decided to put the Mac aside and enjoy a rare, pleasurable cinematic experience today from my perch at seat 10H, 31,000 feet above the Atlantic Ocean.

The basic premise of *The Last Holiday* is by no means new. Many movies have based their plots on the fact that we tend to live our lives with reckless abandon only if we know our days are numbered. Of course, we always know our days are numbered, but that doesn't count, I guess, simply because we don't know what the number is.

The idea of "living every day as if it were your last," as often expounded by all sorts of enlightenment gurus, insists that we make a mistake by not doing what we enjoy; that sacrificing today for the sake of tomorrow is misguided, since we really don't know if there actually is a tomorrow in store for us. Yet, if tomorrow does come, then we were wise to sacrifice today for it. So what are we supposed to do, play the probabilities?

Life is, I guess, like one of those model cars you used to build as a kid—those with the plastic pieces that needed to be twisted off the rectangular panels they came connected to. Except, there is no picture on the box, so you don't know what you are supposed to make. No instructions either, of course. Just a box of plastic pieces. They can make many different things, and depending on what you choose to make, you may have many pieces left over, or not enough pieces to complete your project. Maybe you will choose to make something you will not have time to finish, or maybe you will finish what you choose to make and still have time left over. In the case of the latter, maybe you will have enough pieces left over to build something else. Or maybe not. Complicating matters further, some of the pieces you receive are not visible to you initially; they only become visible under certain, unpredictable circumstances. And some of the pieces you do see may disappear at any time.

So, what do you do, try to build something simple quickly, to make sure you will at least finish something before your time is up? Or do you try to build something more complex, gambling that you will have the time to finish it? Do you use up some of your valuable time to meticulously analyze all the possibilities, or do you build the first thing you are able to discern? Whatever you do, Billy Joel might say, "You may be wrong, but oh, oh, oh you may be right . . . ."

So you build, never knowing if you've made the right choice. But hey, as long as you enjoy the everyday construction process, does it really matter?

Sportsmanship

June 26, 2006

LONG AGO, THE river of cynicism that flows with increasing volume through my mind washed away my passion for spectator sports.

I grew up a rabid soccer fan, as do most kids in Colombia, and cared deeply about the fortunes of my hometown team. Once permanently established in the U.S., I easily shifted my fanaticism to the NBA, NFL, and Major League Baseball, first in Boston, where I spent my college years, and later in South Florida, which has been my home for the past 24 years.

But sometime during the mid-nineties my interest in sports metamorphosed from genuine care for wins and losses to more of a jaundiced, detached, sociological curiosity. These days I am much more interested in understanding the forces that motivate people to care so much about sports than in anything related to the sports themselves. Like, for example, the fascinating fact that people who refuse to pay to watch bad teams perform are thought of as "lousy fans" and are constantly chastised by sports journalists and pundits, when in any other business, these are educated consumers behaving as they should in a capitalistic environment.

However, throughout my sports fan years as well as my more recent sardonic era, I have always felt passionate about sportsmanship. Simple acts, such as a player helping an opposing player up after a rough play, or spectators showering an opposing pitcher with warm applause as he leaves the field after a strong performance, have always warmed my heart in ways a slam dunk or home run never could. When a crowd in Miami applauds the New York Jet that gets up after being hurt, for example, they are elevating their consciousness from the contrived world of the NFL to the real world, where they are glad to know that a fellow human being is OK.

This week our hometown Miami Heat won the NBA championship. But the image that stayed with me after watching championship-defining Game Six, played in Dallas, was not series MVP Dwayne Wade relentlessly driving to the basket, nor 'Zo Mourning rising high to block a shot. Nor was it the relieved face of Heat coach Pat Riley, finally delivering on his promise to bring a championship to Miami. It wasn't even the aforementioned Wade irrationally thanking God for the victory. (I guess the entity in charge simply likes Dwayne more than Dirk.)

No, my mind's official memory of Game Six will feature the crass fans at Dallas's American Airlines Center. (Interestingly, the Miami Heat plays its home games at the American Airlines Arena, making this the first corporate sweep of an NBA Finals series.) The game over, NBA Commissioner David Stern was awarding the Larry O'Brien trophy to the Heat. But instead of the polite silence that common courtesy called for during the Commissioner's remarks (which, of course, included praise for the hometown Mavericks' excellent season) the few fans that had not simply left the building engaged in an embarrassing barrage of boos and catcalls that made Stern's presentation, and the acceptance speeches by Riley and Heat owner Mickey Arison, almost unintelligible.

I don't watch enough sporting events these days to know whether the Dallas fans' appalling performance is indicative of today's sports fans or an isolated event. But after a hard-fought series, with no bad blood or controversy, if the best we can do for the presentation of the league's championship trophy to the team that won it fair and square is an almost empty arena and astounding rudeness from the few remaining fans, I guess Commissioner Stern and his professional franchise owner brethren have succeeded: their fans stay within the confines of the contrived world they have carefully constructed for them even after the game is over. No elevation of consciousness here, folks. Sportsmanship nowhere to be seen.

This week I should have been proud of my team. Instead, I was embarrassed for my species.

TWREoHID

July 3, 2006

THIS WEEK'S RANDOM evidence of humanity's impending downfall:

At least 90 former officials at the Department of Homeland Security now work as executives, consultants, or lobbyists for companies that sell billions of dollars worth of goods and services to their former agency.

Source: The New York Times

A former judge in Bristow, Oklahoma was convicted of exposing himself by using a sexual device while he presided over court cases.

Source: Associated Press

Forty-eight percent of Americans between 18 and 29 have either a tattoo or a piercing.

Source: Associated Press

To attract tourist dollars, in the 1990s Nepal lifted its restrictions on climbing Mount Everest. Amateur adventurers now routinely pay more than $60,000 to commercial companies to be led to the top. Perhaps predictably, the traditional moral code of mountaineering has eroded, and amateurs who have paid a fortune for the bragging rights of reaching the summit will do anything it takes to get there, including actually abandoning dying climbers. "Passing people who are dying is not uncommon," says Ed Viesturs, who has climbed all 14 of the world's 8,000-meter peaks, "Unfortunately, there are those who say, 'It's not my problem. I've spent all this money, and I'm going to the summit.'"

Source: The Week

Angry fans are mounting a class-action suit against Barbara Streisand for coming out of retirement. The irate fans bought expensive tickets for her last tour, which Streisand guaranteed would be her last.

Source: The Week

New York City was declared the most polite city in the world (Zurich, Switzerland was second) by researchers from *Reader's Digest* magazine.

Source: Reader's Digest

The hip-hop fashion of enormously baggy, beltless men's pants has been a boon to law enforcement. Police departments around the country report that young male suspects have become much easier to catch because they trip over their own trousers.

Source: The Wall Street Journal

Artist David Hensel submitted a sculpture to the Royal Academy in London to be considered for display at a top gallery. The sculpture, a human head, was sent separately from its base, a block of slate topped by a small piece of wood. Unaware that one of the parts was only the base for the other, the two parts were judged independently. The head was rejected. The base was thought to have merit and was accepted.

Source: The Week

Net Neutrality

July 9, 2006

MUCH HAS BEEN said lately about the concept of Net Neutrality (NN), a set of rules that would require Internet service providers (ISPs) to manage all Internet traffic on equal terms. NN proponents argue that if ISPs are allowed to charge differently for or block traffic that contains specific content, or originates from a particular source, they will use that power in nefarious ways.

For example, if your ISP is Comcast, it is conceivable that, without NN rules in place, they could roll out a streaming movie service and block your access to movies downloaded or streamed from other sources. Or, if your ISP is AT&T, they may charge you more for using your broadband connection for voice-over-IP (VoIP) services provided by third parties, such as Vonage, in order to promote their own Internet telephony products. ISPs could charge companies for "premium" email delivery services, whereby their messages would be guaranteed to avoid spam filtering and reach their intended recipients in a given amount of time, to the conceivable detriment of individuals and businesses opting not to pay for the premium service.

Many people and many companies, Comcast and AT&T unsurprisingly among them, argue that government regulation of the Internet should not be permitted at all, but that market forces alone should dictate the Internet's evolution. If you are not happy with the way in which your ISP manages your Internet connection, they say, switch ISPs. And that would make sense, except that the way that broadband has evolved in the U.S., our connection to the Internet is typically controlled by regulated monopolies, and competition is not exactly the norm. Typically, we have a grand total of two choices when it comes to broadband Internet access: cable or DSL. And in many rural areas, the notion of choosing among ISPs is laughable; people consider themselves fortunate to have broadband access at all.

Companies like Comcast and AT&T also like to bring up the point that they have financed the infrastructure investment involved with connecting our homes, through fiber and copper, to the so-called backbones that constitute the Internet's main thoroughfares. They feel they should be able to reap the benefits of their investment. However, they made the investment while acting as legally protected monopolies, and their rates for long distance telephone calls and cable television service were not subject to competitive pressures.

NN is, no doubt, a complicated issue. Vested interests abound, technical issues must be clearly understood, and any decisions reached will affect us all for years to come. So, who are the brilliant minds charged with making these tough decisions? Politicians, of course. People like U.S. Senator Ted Stevens (R-Alaska), the chairman of the Senate Commerce Committee, who demonstrated his mastery of the subject matter last week as he explained why he voted against an amendment inserting basic net neutrality provisions into a pending telecommunications bill. The Chairman's words:

> There's one company now you can sign up and you can get a movie delivered to your house daily by delivery service. OK. And currently it comes to your house, it gets put in the mailbox when you get

home and you change your order but you pay for that, right.

But this service is now going to go through the Internet and what you do is you just go to a place on the Internet and you order your movie and guess what you can order ten of them delivered to you and the delivery charge is free.

Ten of them streaming across that Internet and what happens to your own personal Internet?

I just the other day got, an Internet was sent by my staff at 10 o'clock in the morning on Friday and I just got it yesterday. Why?

Because it got tangled up with all these things going on on the Internet commercially.

So you want to talk about the consumer? Let's talk about you and me. We use this Internet to communicate and we aren't using it for commercial purposes.

We aren't earning anything by going on that Internet. Now I'm not saying you have to or you want to discriminate against those people.

The regulatory approach is wrong. Your approach is regulatory in the sense that it says, "No one can charge anyone for massively invading this world of the Internet." No, I'm not finished. I want people to understand my position, I'm not going to take a lot of time.

They want to deliver vast amounts of information over the Internet. And again, the Internet is not something you just dump something on. It's not a truck.

It's a series of tubes.

And if you don't understand those tubes can be filled and if they are filled, when you put your message in, it gets in line and its going to be delayed by anyone that puts into that tube enormous amounts of material, enormous amounts of material.

Now we have a separate Department of Defense Internet now, did you know that?

Do you know why?

Because they have to have theirs delivered immediately. They can't afford getting delayed by other people.

Now I think these people are arguing whether they should be able to dump all that stuff on the Internet ought to consider if they should develop a system themselves.

Maybe there is a place for a commercial net but it's not using what consumers use every day.

It's not using the messaging service that is essential to small businesses, to our operation of families.

The whole concept is that we should not go into this until someone shows that there is something that has been done that really is a violation of net neutrality that hits you and me.

Listening to or reading Senator Stevens's remarks is about as pleasant as taking a deep whiff of freshly stepped-on cat doo-doo. And, lest we forget, as the longest-serving Republican currently in the Senate, Stevens is actually the current president pro tempore, which makes him number three in the order of presidential succession. Yes, my fellow Americans, if President Bush, Vice President Cheney, and Speaker of the House John Hastert should find themselves, say, golfing together next Sunday morning and are suddenly abducted by a band of Venusian extremists, my eight-year old son would have a better understanding of the Internet than the President of the United States. (Well, that may be the case even without the Venusians' intervention, for that matter.)

Although we at Sifter Stickers are not particularly fond of agreeing with shotgun pundit and confessed Mac baiter John C. Dvorak, in this particular case we do agree with the cranky columnist. We are, as Dvorak recently ranted, living in the Golden Age of the Internet. We will soon find out that the open, free Network of Networks is really too good to be true. In the hands of Senator Stevens and his clueless, lobbyist fodder ilk, we are headed toward a restricted and blocked Internet, where the quality of our access to content and services is determined by others with interests different from, and frequently in direct conflict with, our own.

Enjoy the free, neutral Internet, dear reader. It will soon be a relic we fondly remember.

Update

On January 3, 2007, the 110th Congress convened, and as the Democrats took control of the chamber, Robert Byrd replaced Ted Stevens as President pro tem—and as such, third in the line of presidential succession after Vice President Dick Cheney and Speaker of the House Nancy Pelosi. I am not familiar with Mr. Byrd's grasp of the Internet, but one can only assume it's a step up from Mr. Stevens's!

As far as other parts of the essay are concerned, as I revisit it almost two years later, it seems little has changed. Comcast has admitted to "slowing down" BitTorrent traffic, and evidence has been presented that various ISPs, Comcast included, actually routinely shut down BitTorrents during peak hours. Yet there has also been news about Comcast and BitTorrent actually joining forces. Comcast and AT&T argue that they must somehow control Internet traffic to make sure that bandwidth is preserved for all users, and not simply hogged by the few that constantly download and stream video. Consumers who want to use their Internet connection for such downloads complain that their traffic is *(continues)* unfairly slowed down and blocked. In my view, the only fair way for users to actually get what they pay for is to change the current unlimited, flat fee approach to Internet access and replace it with a variable model where consumers actually pay for the bandwidth they use, like they do for electricity or water. Metered Internet access is an admittedly unpopular approach, but represents the only way I can think of where all interests are served fairly.

To Do or Not To Do

July 17, 2006

THERE ARE FEW things as satisfying as crossing an item off a to-do list. That magical stroke of the pen (or click of the mouse, more likely) represents a tangible accomplishment. Success. Winning. Fulfillment. One less thing to worry about. One more thing to feel good about. Triumph, indeed.

During the past few years, I've tried to model my own to-do lists on David Allen's seminal "Getting Things Done" approach, where, among many other techniques, Allen suggests categorizing to-do items contextually, in order to make the best use of the resources available to you at any given time. For example, one category could be "Online," where you would include all items that require an Internet connection to be completed. Another category, "Phone," perhaps, would contain items that could be knocked off if you have a few spare minutes with only your cell phone available. The idea is to match the to-do item with the proper context, thus avoiding the inefficiency of going through your entire to-do list in order to identify items that you are able to complete at any given time. You simply look at the items in whichever category matches your resource availability.

So, your to-do list is subdivided by context. Now, at any given time and in any given context, you are able to easily identify to-do items that you can get done and satisfyingly cross off your list. And therein, dear reader, lies the problem.

A properly managed, contextually organized to-do list makes it easy for you to always find items to cross off, regardless of where you are and what resources you have available. So, where's the problem, you ask? Well, an inevitable byproduct of a well-managed to-do list is the feeling that if you are not engaged in an activity that will result in a crossed-off item, you are by definition wasting time. Sort of like cuddling, as opposed to sex, in the sense of an activity without a definitive culmination. And unless your to-do list includes items such as "spending a Sunday afternoon with your family at the beach," or "kicking a soccer ball around with your son," or "sitting in thoughtful silence," or even "sharing intimate moments with the person you love," then those activities, surely among the most important activities in life, may easily become victims of the almighty to-do list.

David Allen argues that only by clearing your mind of the things you need to do by putting them down on paper (or, more likely, a hard disk somewhere) will you achieve the peace of mind necessary to truly relax, become productive, and perhaps be able to spend more time involved in the "off-the-list" activities that life is really all about. But in the age of pervasive connectivity (did we just coin a phrase?), the difficulty lies in identifying the proper times to simply put the to-do list aside, and indulge in activities that will not, alas, result in the orgasmic checkmark, realizing that those activities are perhaps the reason for the to-do list to exist in the first place.

And neither the undoubtedly gifted David Allen nor anyone else will help us with that one, dear reader. Clearly, to do or not to do is up to you.

Communism and Youth

July 23, 2006

MY GRANDFATHER JOE used to say, and I'm paraphrasing here, "A person who never contemplates communism during his youth has no heart, but a person who is not a capitalist as an adult has no brain." Harsh words, to be sure, but as in everything Joe used to say, there is wisdom to be found there.

In the outstanding 2004 movie *The Motorcycle Diaries*, a twenty-something Ernesto "Che" Guevara is portrayed as a gifted, compassionate medical student who is transformed by his experiences on a 1952 cross-continental road trip with friend Alberto Granado. During the 12,000-kilometer trip, which took Guevara and Granado from their home town of Buenos Aires down to the Argentinean pampas, back up through Chile, Peru, Colombia, and finally Venezuela, Guevara is exposed to the colossal injustices rampant in the South America of his day, injustices sadly still rampant over 50 years later. And whether one is on a motorcycle trip through the Peruvian hinterlands in 1952 or simply driving the streets of 2006 Bogota, as I often do, it is impossible not to bristle at the contrast between those who have it all and those who have nothing. And it is impossible not to want to do something about it, not to want to somehow cure the unfairness of it all.

And communism, of course, seems to be the magic bullet. From each according to his abilities, the doctrine goes, and to each according to his need. Everyone happy. Imagine all the people, sharing all the world. But wait, Mr. Lennon, it's just not that simple.

I think the reason my grandfather felt that adults would somehow "grow out" of communism is that as the idealism of youth graduates into the cynicism of maturity, we realize that human beings are a greedy, selfish lot, and although there are many notable exceptions, we pretty much focus on our own needs and the needs of those close to us first. And so it follows that capitalism works (and communism doesn't) because of the way human beings are. So although as we mature we neither lose our yearning for fairness nor our hatred of injustice, we simply realize that life is unfair because of human nature. Greed trumps compassion every day of the week, most likely as a consequence of evolution. And so, we are left with the realization that communism will not cure injustice, but simply reshape it. And maybe when we are young we simply haven't seen enough of human nature to arrive at this unfortunate yet inescapable conclusion.

To put it succinctly, communism is the perfect system for the species that we would like to be. Capitalism is the system best suited to the species that we actually are. And that, dear reader, is certainly nothing to brag about.

TWREoHID II

July 18, 2006

THIS WEEK'S RANDOM evidence of humanity's impending downfall (Volume 2):

Nearly 60 percent of U.S. homeowners don't have enough insurance to rebuild if their home is destroyed in a hurricane or other natural disaster.

Source: USA Today

Telemarketers have barraged the top-secret Homeland Security hotline with calls, forcing the government to place the number on the National Do Not Call Registry. The secret hotline is supposed to connect the federal government to the governors of the 50 states in the event of an emergency. But, says Governor Ruth Ann Miner of Delaware, "Every time that phone rings, it's a telemarketer." Wisconsin Governor Jim Doyle says that when the hotline phone rang in the early days of the Iraq war, he grabbed it in panic only to have someone ask him if he was happy with his long distance service.

Source: The Week

A community swimming club in Fairfax, Virginia can no longer afford the insurance premiums on its 3-meter diving board, so it's coming down, as are thousands more across the country. Turns out that even though diving boards are implicated in fewer than 20 of the over 50,000 annual pool-related injuries and deaths in the U.S., lawyers pounce on the diving board incidents, routinely winning awards of $5 million or more, even when no one is negligent. The payoffs inflate every pool's insurance costs, and ultimately force many of them to simply take down the diving board.

Source: The Wall Street Journal

In 2002, House Speaker Dennis Hastert of Illinois and two partners bought 196 acres of land near Plano, Illinois that was largely landlocked, with no major access roads. Hastert soon began pushing to build a highway nearby; during the summer of 2005 he personally intervened to "earmark" two appropriations that gave $207 million to build a highway and interchange just five miles away. When the acreage was sold to a developer that December, Hastert reaped a $1.8 million profit. Hastert's lawyers insist there is nothing unlawful about this transaction. The sad news is, they're right.

Source: The Chicago Tribune

The average American now has just two close friends, a new study has found. One in four people say they have no close friends.

Source: USA Today

A congressional candidate in Utah blamed "the devil" for setbacks that saw him lose a primary election. Republican John Jacob told the *Salt Lake Tribune* that Satan himself had caused a string of setbacks that hampered his ability to fund his campaign.

Source: The Week

Despite the exodus from New Orleans residents caused by hurricane Katrina, business at Louisiana's casinos is booming, apparently fueled by relief workers earning big paychecks.

Source: The Associated Press

About 30 percent of high school term papers are plagiarized, in whole or in part, from the Internet.

Source: The Los Angeles Times

An Argentinean soccer fan miraculously rose from his wheelchair in excitement during his team's World Cup victory over the Netherlands. It turned out the man and two friends were pretending to be disabled simply to obtain cheap tickets to the game. All three were ejected.

Source: The Week

Litmus Test

August 5, 2006

ULTRA-SUAVE GANGSTER Sonny (his last name is never mentioned), brilliantly played by Chazz Palminteri in *A Bronx Tale* (1993), maintains that it's easy to determine if a woman is a keeper. All you need to do is subject her to a simple test. In Sonny's words, "You pull up right where she lives, right? Before you get outta the car, you lock both doors. Then, get outta the car, you walk over to her. You bring her over to the car. Dig out the key, put it in the lock and open the door for her. Then you let her get in. Then you close the door. Then you walk around the back of the car and look through the rear window. If she doesn't reach over and lift up that button so that you can get in: dump her." It's as simple as that.

So young Calogero "C" Anello took Sonny's advice, and subjected the object of his desires to "the test." That night, upon picking her up for their date, he gracefully opened the passenger door of his car for her, and lovingly guided her into her seat. He then strolled to the back of the car, and peered into the rear window as he ambled across to the driver's side. The moment of truth. A palpable hush came over the theater, as the audience held its collective breath. Will she or won't she? Then, relief. The young woman elegantly leaned over toward the driver's door, and thrust a provocatively bare arm toward the 1960s-style plunger lock. In a titillating display of balance and grace, she extended her index and middle fingers, inserted them gently under the protruding brim of the plunger, and, in one fluid motion, raised her entire forearm, bringing the plunger up with it. Door unlocked. Test passed. Flying colors. C stepped in and sat down, and while his ass was firmly on the leatherette, his head was somewhere in the clouds, and his stomach was in beautiful downtown Flutterville. The collective sigh from the audience completed the effect. The movie could have ended right there.

Ah, the simple test. All the complexities of life distilled into an easily measurable result. In an unpredictable world of cruel uncertainty, nothing is more reassuring than a litmus test. Dip the magic paper in. Red means acid, blue means alkaline. No arguments. No doubts.

From the petals of a daisy to an alphabet soup of standardized tests, from horoscopes to bell curves, we all strive to find simple ways to predict complex behavior. With varying degrees of success, we attempt to understand what makes things happen, and then take all the variables involved and somehow compress them into a simple, yet effective predictor. And then we go on and use these predictors to make all sorts of decisions, once again with widely varying degrees of success.

The virtues of a woman are, alas, a bit more difficult to measure than the acidity of a liquid. And despite Sonny's assurances, C's earnest acceptance and the entire theater audience's joyous suspension of disbelief, C's prospects for long-term happiness do not really hinge on his girl's momentary display of common courtesy. And yet, does that really matter? Or is it the moment that matters? The butterflies. Sonny lovingly architected a foundation of passion for C to build upon. A self-fulfilling prophesy, perhaps. A predictor with daisy-petal accuracy, but just enough plausibility to make it work on an emotional level.

Truth is, there is no simple yet effective way to predict the future behavior of a human being. So it seems best to instead simply enjoy its discovery. By embracing the allure of everyday kindness. And feeling the butterflies when she unlocks the door.

WWDC Keynote
August 13, 2006

I T'S A COMFORTABLE 59° F in San Francisco at 5:30 A.M., as the crowd begins to assemble outside Moscone West. I'm lucky to be among the first to arrive; there are only about 20 people ahead of me. There will be over 4,800 people behind me four hours later.

The camaraderie is instant and genuine in line. Differences that tragically are thought to be important away from Moscone melt away to leave the only thing that should be important everywhere: as a King once said, the content of our character. We share anecdotes and muffins.

The outside doors open at 7:30, exactly. We are herded to our second staging area near the giant escalators on the far end of the first floor of the hangar-like structure, where astoundingly fast wireless awaits those lucky enough to have the newest equipment. Many sit crossed-legged on the floor, laptops open, working, playing. I am one of them. People keep streaming in.

Once-a-year friends greet each other with genuine warmth. Veterans share experiences with rookies. Speculation runs rampant; last-minute predictions are made. Pundits wax philosophical. Skeptics debunk.

Around 8 we are herded up the escalators and snaked around the cavernous hallways of Moscone West's second floor, the line making three sides of a giant square around the block of conference rooms. Once again we sit, enjoying the blazing Internet connection, the easy conversation. At this point many of us have been standing in line for two and a half hours. Nobody complains.

At 9:30 we are allowed to walk (no running, please) over to the second-floor escalators. We ride them up to the third floor, and enter the Promised Land. We take the best seat we can find, outside, of course, of the first section, reserved for VIPs. My group is in the second row of the second section, a glorious place to be.

Once the keynote is over, its content, form, and every nuance will be subjected to thorough analysis. Wall-Streeters will modify targets, pundits will opine. And I will once again be awed. For although Barnum and Bailey may feel otherwise, I know the truth. A Steve Jobs keynote is, clearly, the Greatest Show on Earth.

And those thirty minutes, between 9:30 and 10:00, when the lining up is over, all obstacles are defeated, and 5000 souls bask in sweet anticipation. . . . I'll put it this way: if I were to get up, leave the room, and fly back home the instant before Jobs confidently bounds up the stairs leading to the stage, I will go home happy and satisfied. For I have been part of a rare and wonderful thing.

The Chasm

September 10, 2006

REFERRING TO ASSEMBLYWOMAN Bonnie Garcia, California Governor Arnold Schwarzenegger said, "She maybe is Puerto Rican or the same thing as Cuban. I mean, they are all very hot. They have the, you know, part of the black blood in them and part of the Latino blood in them that together makes it." The remarks were made during a casual conversation Schwarzenegger had with top aides at a private meeting last spring, a conversation that was, unbeknownst to Mr. Schwarzenegger, recorded by a staff member. The Los Angeles Times obtained a copy of the audio recording last week, and promptly published the governor's remarks on its Web site last Thursday evening, as well as in Friday's newspaper.

Predictably, the governor apologized for his remarks the day they appeared on the morning paper, saying that he "cringed" after reading his own words.

Whether it's Governor Schwarzenegger presenting his analysis of ethnicity and race as they relate to temperament, or actor Mel Gibson expressing his views on Judaism to a roadside audience of one (to then, of course, profusely apologize the next day), there seems to be a big difference between what people really think and what they would like others to think that they think. And although this phenomenon seems to be more prevalent among politicians and celebrities, it really applies to everyone, except no one really cares about what non-famous people really think—unless it's embarrassing, provocative, or both.

But what's interesting to me is neither that Governor Schwarzenegger was caught by a covert recording, nor that alcohol made Mr. Gibson more, ahem, forthcoming about his views. What I find fascinating is the deep chasm that exists between the way people present themselves to be and the way they really are. Does the chasm represent the depth of our feelings of inadequacy? Does it illustrate the severity of the gap between our idealism and our reality? Or is it simply a matter of hypocrisy, or let us say "marketing": I'm happy with who I am, but I need people to think I'm different in order to (a) get elected; (b) get into her pants; (c) succeed in whatever my goal is?

In any event, the size of the chasm represents the degree of difference between an individual's public persona and her "real," private character. It would be great if we could somehow discern the size of people's chasms, or, shall we say, their Chasm Depth Factor (CDF), in order to understand how comfortable they are in their own skin, how good they feel about themselves and how honestly they portray themselves to others. People like, say, disgraced televangelist Jim Bakker would have an extremely high CDF, and I would speculate that someone like rocker Bruce Springsteen would have a CDF close to zero. George W. Bush: high CDF. Late former President Ronald Reagan: probably a low CDF, despite being an actor by training. I somehow always felt Reagan was simply being himself all those years—or maybe he was a much better actor than his Hollywood career would indicate. Who knows? See, that's why we need public CDFs!

"Life," said Forrest Gump, as played by the amazing Tom Hanks, "is like a box of chocolates . . . you never know what you're gonna get." When is comes to people, though, the analogy is not quite right. For although the outside of the chocolates does not necessarily reveal their content, at least they don't deliberately present themselves as one thing while really being something else entirely.

They Should Pay

September 20, 2006

YOU MAY HAVE experienced a post-9/11 NSCBRD (No-Show Checked Bag Removal Delay), the airline flight delay that occurs when a passenger who has checked luggage for a flight does not board the aircraft, forcing the airline to locate the no-show's bags and remove them from the cargo hold before the flight is allowed to proceed. The idea, obviously, is that a checked bag without a corresponding passenger is an implied security threat. I've experienced NSCBRD events lasting anywhere from 20 minutes to a couple of hours or so. I wonder, though, if offending passengers are fined or penalized in any way for inconveniencing a planeload of people due to their carelessness.

We at Sifter Stickers firmly believe that people who cause NSCBRDs should be heavily fined, and moreover would like to implement a system whereby the following individuals are also charged a significant penalty for behavior which ranges from callously selfish to mildly disturbing to simply puzzling:

- People who make multiple travel reservations with the intention of using only one of them but wanting to secure various choices for themselves at the expense of others.
- People who cut in line. Any line.
- Parents who act as if the fate of the civilized world hinges upon the result of their eight-year-old's soccer game.
- Men who wear monogrammed shirts, whether on the chest pocket, sleeve, or anywhere else. Exactly what is the point?
- People who believe that airline flight boarding sequences do not apply to them.
- Families who affix stickers with cartoon figures representing family members to the rear window of their SUVs. Why would anyone (except maybe kidnappers, thieves or perverts) be interested in knowing that the family includes a mom, a dad, a soccer-playing son, a ballerina daughter, a dog, and two cats?
- People who constantly distribute and redistribute sappy, feel-good PowerPoint presentations.
- Airline personnel who stand at airport security checkpoints directing passengers whose departure times are imminent to the front of the line, thus rewarding and promoting the late-arriving passengers' irresponsible behavior while penalizing those who make an effort to arrive at the airport in a timely manner.
- People who impose their beliefs on others, or who believe those who don't share their beliefs are somehow inferior or unenlightened.
- Non-military personnel who drive Hummers.
- People who order a Big Mac, fries, and a Diet Coke. Hey, why not supersize, and add a Slim-Fast shake?

Stubborn Futility
October 4, 2006

FIDEL CASTRO WILL die an old and happy man. And as he reaches the end of his existence, I'm sure he'll chuckle as he thinks about all the Cuban exiles in Miami who for so long refused to accept the ineffectiveness of the United States' policy of embargo, and instead continued to demand its enforcement despite overwhelming evidence of its colossal failure. But the blind stubbornness of the Cuban exiles pales in comparison to the astonishingly futile perseverance of those endowed with religious faith.

The amazing irrationality of worship in general is made evident by even a cursory look at any religion's prayer books. God is repeatedly praised and thanked for watching over humanity, healing the sick, helping the poor, and so on. Apparently, those who so fervently chant these words have not taken a look at the world around them. News flash: often, the sick do not heal. There are millions of desperately poor people all over the world. According to the United Nations, 2.6 billion people in the world lack access to basic sanitation. Violence abounds. Good people suffer and die. Children are molested. All sorts of calamities befall decent folk. Yet people worship God, praise him incessantly, and look to him for help and guidance. Help and guidance that never arrive.

During the Passover Seder, it is a Jewish tradition to leave an empty chair for the prophet Elijah, in case he shows up for dinner. He's been a no-show for 5,766 straight years, but still, the chair is left vacant for him every Passover, seemingly as a symbol of our stubborn naïveté. The empty chair, like the emptiness of prayers unanswered, stands as a stark reminder of things that refuse to happen regardless of how many times we employ ineffective techniques to bring them about.

We humans seem to value the warm comfort of familiarity over the cold logic of rationality with the blind perseverance of moths flying into the fire. Seeing their friends and neighbors suddenly incinerated somehow does not stop the hapless moths from barreling to their deaths, as inescapable evidence of ineffectiveness stops neither the Cuban exiles from promoting the ill-conceived embargo, nor the faithful from worshiping and praying.

Maybe someday a moth will suddenly experience a Eureka moment and boldly turn back from the fire, inspiring millions of colleagues. And maybe someday a family will decide to dust off Elijah's chair during a Seder, and invite a person in genuine need to sit down and enjoy the abundance so prevalent at those events. Should the prophet Elijah show up, well, there's always room for one more!

TSA

November 1, 2006

RECENT SCENES FROM a U.S. airport (I am not making this up):

"Sir, do you have any liquids, gels or pastes to declare?"

"Yes, I have a toiletry bag with various liquids, gels and pastes, all within the mandated 3-ounce limit."

"But are they in a Ziploc, see-through plastic bag?"

"No, they're in my toiletry bag. Would you like to inspect them?"

"No. If they are not in a Ziploc, see-through plastic bag, you will need to either place them in checked baggage or surrender them."

"But, what difference does it make if they're in a Ziploc bag if you are able to inspect them?"

"The difference between allowing you to carry them on board or not."

"OK, I do have this see-through, zippered bag that I could put them in."

"Is it a Ziploc?"

"No, it's a zippered, see-through cosmetics bag."

"It needs to be Ziploc. It cannot be zippered."

"Why?"

"Ask George W. I don't come up with these rules, I just enforce them."

(Same place, 45 minutes later)

"OK, I found someone with an extra Ziploc bag who was nice enough to let me have it! I've stood in line all over again, and here I am, declaring my liquids, gels and pastes, this time in a regulation Ziploc, see-through bag!"

"Sir, that is a gallon-sized bag. It needs to be a quart-sized Ziploc bag."

"You must be joking."

"Do I look like Jay Leno?"

"Quart-sized, huh? I'll be back."

(Same place, 30 minutes later)

"OK, I was able to obtain a quart-sized Ziploc see-through bag."

"OK sir, let me take a look. Sir, this tube of toothpaste is labeled 5 ounces. That's over the limit."

"Yes, but it is almost completely used up! You can clearly see that it's rolled up almost to the top. There can't be more than one ounce of paste in there!"

"Ah, but that's not the rule. The container must be labeled '3 ounces' or less."

"But, doesn't the rule state that you cannot take more than 3 ounces of liquid or paste on board? I'm taking less than 3 ounces!"

"But the container is labeled 5 ounces, so you must surrender your toothpaste."

"OK, take my toothpaste!"

"No sir, I am not taking your toothpaste. You are surrendering it."

"OK, I hereby surrender my toothpaste."

"Thank you, sir. Enjoy your flight!"

Moral of the Story: Obsessively early airport arrivals occasionally save the day!

Ringtones

November 10, 2006

ACCORDING TO BMI, a major performing rights organization that represents songwriters, composers, and music publishers, the U.S. ringtone market is expected to exceed $600 million in sales this year. Music market tracker Billboard estimates global ringtone sales racked up $4.4 billion in 2005. Baskerville/Informa Media projects that mobile ringtones will account for more than 12 percent of global music industry revenues by 2008.

Ringtones! The song snippets used to customize the ringing of cell phones! $4.4 billion! I have but one question: why?

The overwhelming popularity of ringtones seems baffling, primarily for the following two reasons:

Reason #1. Pre-teenagers and teenagers form the bulk of the ringtone market. Yet this is the same demographic that brought the music industry to its knees by reshaping the way in which they acquire music! The combination of the unabashed greed of the recording industry and ubiquitous broadband Internet connections spawned Napster, Limewire, and their ilk, fueling the notion among kids that music is meant to be freely shared, not paid for. So they simply stopped purchasing CDs. When Steve Jobs finally got the music labels to come to their senses and embrace technology instead of pathetically fighting against it, creating Apple's iTunes/iPod juggernaut, at least a portion of downloaded music became legit. However, even today most teenagers eschew the silky elegance and consistent quality of the iTunes Store and instead continue to roam the seamy underbelly of music sales: illegal downloads.

OK, so let's get this straight: most kids today would rather put up with all sorts of spyware, the threat of viruses, halting, stop-and-go downloads, and inconsistent quality than pony up 99 cents for a superb user experience, pristine files, and good karma. Yet these same kids pay anywhere from $1 to $3 for a snippet of a song, to be heard only when their cell phone rings? They could have the entire song for $0.99! And listen to it at their leisure on their iPod! Inexplicable. Downright absurd.

Reason #2: When the phone rings, you need to make a decision. Answer or ignore. So the perfect notification mechanism for a phone call is a differentiated, unobtrusive sound that alerts you to the fact that the phone is ringing, and then allows you to make your decision in peace. Actually enjoying the sound the phone makes hinders the whole operation! If you intend to answer, do you delay answering to enjoy a few more notes of the song, and run the risk that you will wait too long and the call will go to voicemail? Ignoring the call implies that you are otherwise occupied. So do you stop what you are doing to listen to the song, only to be rudely shocked by the snippet's premature termination? If you have an iPod, you can listen to whatever song you want, whenever you want to. Setting a song you like as your ringtone condemns it to become annoying to you; it's only a matter of time.

Do teenagers need to assert their individuality so much that they resort to such absurdities as ringtones? Do they think that by selecting the right ringtone they will be considered cool by their peers?

I think it goes a bit deeper. It is a fact of life that human beings crave attention; we're just wired that way. We all want to carve out niches for ourselves. I publish a blog and produce a podcast. My 15-year-old daughter maintains a MySpace page, and downloads what she thinks are cool ringtones. She balks at paying for music, but has no problem shelling out the big bucks for "accessories"—and that is what ringtones have become. So even though ringtones are, in a way, a subset of music, in another way they are not. They are a part of your style, as much an adornment as body piercing or tattoos. They help paint the picture of who you are.

Limewire and $2.50 ringtones. A baffling combination? No, simply another window into the fascinatingly complex human soul.

Update

Interestingly, ringtone sales are beginning to decline. BMI estimates U.S. ringtone sales for 2008 will total $510 million, representing a 15% drop from 2006, which happened to be the year the U.S. ringtone market peaked at $600 million. Ringback tones (music that a caller hears on the other end while a call is connecting), though, may make up the difference: BMI expects ringback tones to hit $210 million in the U.S. this year.

Zune

November 29, 2006

SHOULD WE PITY the poor, pathetic Zune, or should we fear its descendants?

You may be asking exactly why should we pity Microsoft's recent attempt at a so-called iPod killer? Allow me to count the reasons: The Zune has Wi-Fi! How cool! But wait, can you sync the Zune wirelessly with a computer? No. Can you download music to the Zune wirelessly from an online music store? No. Well then, why Wi-Fi at all? To share music with "people in your vicinity"? But if I "beam" (Microsoft uses the somewhat racy term "squirt") someone a song from my Zune, even if that song came from my own CD, or if it's my own recording and therefore has no digital rights management at all, the Zune will add DRM to it, limiting it to three plays on the squirtee's Zune, or three days' duration, whichever comes first. And the transfer from Zune to Zune is not exactly swift—as Steve Jobs has mentioned, by the time you transfer the song, the girl already left!

1. Inexplicably, the Zune is not compatible with Microsoft's own Windows Media Player software! Makes absolutely no sense, given that Media Player is on every Windows computer, and even on some Macs. No, to use the Zune you must install new software, the Zune Software and Marketplace.
2. Although the Zune's main control mechanism looks suspiciously like the iPod's legendary click wheel, it is merely a disguised rocker switch, much less efficient at navigating an extensive music library.
3. In another twist of bitter irony, the Zune is not compatible with Microsoft's own DRM scheme, PlaysForSure. Microsoft developed this standard and convinced many vendors to adopt it, arguing that it would help simplify matters for users: no matter what music store you purchase your music from, and no matter whose music player you buy, your music will, well, play for sure. So now, Microsoft's own player brings with it a whole new system, with its own DRM scheme, and its own online store. The irony! The betrayal!
4. The new Zune Marketplace does not allow you to simply purchase music with money. In a pathetically transparent attempt to obscure the true cost of music, Microsoft makes you purchase "Zune Points" first, and then purchase music using those points. All of these "funny money" schemes have but one objective: to confuse customers. As opposed to the iPod and the iTunes Store, you can't use the Zune or the Zune Marketplace to subscribe to podcasts (recorded audio or video programs subscribed to using RSS feed technology). I should point out that the term "podcast" is somewhat misleading, since you do *not* need an iPod to subscribe to or listen to a podcast. You may subscribe to audio and video podcasts by using the built-in functionality in iTunes on Windows and Mac OS X, but there are many other podcast subscription applications available on both platforms. And you can listen to

audio podcasts or watch video podcasts on your computer (Windows or Mac), or on any MP3 player (iPod or not). The podcast market is growing significantly, and represents an exciting new paradigm in entertainment consumption. Many people use their music players primarily to listen to audio podcasts and watch video podcasts. But Microsoft's Zune team chose to ignore this exciting trend.

5. The iPod and iTunes Store provide an admirably similar experience on Mac OS X and Windows. The Zune and Zune Marketplace will simply not work on the Mac.

So, the Zune is a pathetic product, destined for quick, unceremonious failure.

But wait . . .

Microsoft has, on many occasions, turned in a pathetic first effort at a product category dominated by others, only to patiently refine and improve the effort into something just about passable, and then used its marketing muscle (as well as questionable marketing strategies) to pound it into market dominance. A great example is Windows itself. About the time that Apple was introducing the groundbreaking Macintosh, Microsoft released Windows 1.0. Nobody cared. In 1987 they released Windows 2.0. It was massively ignored. But in April 1992 Microsoft released Windows 3.1, the first somewhat decent version of their graphical user interface. Windows 3.1 sold more than one million copies within two months of its release. By the time Microsoft released Windows 95 in August 1995, Windows' dominance in the marketplace was clearly established, albeit with a product vastly inferior to even the original Macintosh OS introduced over ten years before.

Do we need to be concerned about Zune 3.1, somewhere on the horizon? Maybe, but in the meantime, we are left to wonder how a company with virtually unlimited resources can come out with such a laughably bad product. Let's hope the folks at Redmond don't end up with the last laugh here, because we will all suffer for it. Let's not forget that in order to appease Universal music, Microsoft agreed to pay Universal a royalty on Zune sales, rumored to be $1 per unit sold, in exchange for licensing recordings for use on its Zune Marketplace download service. Apple has so far admirably avoided giving in to the music labels' unadulterated greed, and that has proved to be invaluable to the consumer, as its DRM scheme (play purchased music on up to five computers and unlimited iPods, burn up to seven CDs with the same playlist) rarely gets in the way of users. Apple has also refused to yield to the music labels' push for variable pricing on songs, keeping the simple 99-cents-per-song price point. If part of Microsoft's strategy is to cozy up to the music labels and help build an environment that is more agreeable to their wishes, the iPod/iTunes environment we all know and love could eventually be in jeopardy.

So, should we pity the poor, pathetic Zune, or should we fear its descendants?

Update

In mid-2008, the answer to that question continues to be that we should pity the pathetic Zune. Although its descendants are a bit more capable than the original Zune, and it truly is, objectively speaking, not a bad piece of hardware (and software, for that matter), it seems like the whole iTunes/iPod ecosystem has evolved to the point of presenting a formidable barrier to entry for a competing product, at least one that is not innovative in any significant way. And Microsoft was never able to build a credible media distribution system around the Zune. It seems that, unlike desktop operating systems or office productivity software suites, the window of opportunity for Microsoft to dominate the portable music player/downloadable music market has firmly closed. In the wake of Microsoft's failed attempt to purchase Yahoo! and the continuing debacle that is Windows Vista, can we now refer to Microsoft as "beleaguered"?

Gerstein

December 4, 2006

I'M NOT SURE exactly why our young men and women are being killed in Iraq, or Afghanistan, or anywhere else. I can't possibly fathom some of our government's decisions. I often doubt the motives of politicians, religious leaders, law enforcement officials, corporate executives—really, almost everyone in a position of power. But I do know one thing. On December 4, 2006, many came to the Richard E. Gerstein Justice Building in Miami as defendants. They were tried for their alleged crimes. And the guilt or innocence of every single one of them was determined by a jury of their peers, exactly as the Constitution mandates.

I know this because I was there.

I was there along with 800 others in the jury pool, although most of us could have gotten out of it if we really tried. Outside of the Richard E. Gerstein Justice Building we each have our own agendas, lives, goals. Preconceived notions. Prejudices. But sometime on the morning of Monday the 4th, I think it was around 9:20, we all realized that, no offense to the hallowed Mr. Gerstein, we were inside a place called Justice. And we were there to administer exactly that. As are the judges, bailiffs, clerks, and staff who spend their work days at creaky, overburdened, decrepit, glorious Gerstein.

Now, anyone who knows me even casually realizes that I'm pretty much a cynic. And yes, I was extremely grateful that I had obtained a shiny new V640 EV-DO card for my MacBook Pro, so I was able to be online at the Jury Assembly Room and knock a few items off my well-heeled to-do list while waiting to be called to voir dire. But the utter fascination I'd experienced the two times I had been to Gerstein before was equaled and actually exceeded this time. Fascination with the glorious obsession for Justice displayed by everyone who is part of the system. A contagious obsession, and one that transforms busy people who just want to get jury duty over with into thoughtful citizens, grateful to live in a society that takes such pains to guarantee that our fates will always be decided by people like us, people who have never met us, people who have no interest in our fate, but act only in the interest of justice. When we step into Gerstein as jurors we are bestowed with the special grandeur that comes from being an integral part of something truly magical. We are the Finders of Fact, the Blindfolded Lady with the Scales. And in the end, all look to us for our pronouncement. Because we are Justice.

We were a pretty diverse group at Gerstein that Monday. All walks of life, different races, ethnic backgrounds (this is South Florida, after all!). But when our right hands were in the air, and the question was whether or not we could be impartial in determining the fate of one of our fellow citizens, we were not thinking of the work that would pile up if we were selected to serve on a jury. We were not thinking of the inconvenience to our families. We were not thinking of the differences among us. We were humbled by the awesome responsibility entrusted to us by the Founding Fathers. And we were thinking of the pride in our hearts and the goose bumps on our arms moments earlier, when, as we followed the bailiff into the courtroom, he shouted. "All rise for the jurors." And all rose for our entrance. Because we are Justice.

TWREoHID III

December 18, 2006

THIS WEEK'S RANDOM Evidence of Humanity's Impending Downfall (Volume 3):

Independence, Missouri prosecutors say a man shoved a cell phone down his girlfriend's throat because he was angry and jealous. But defense attorneys insisted as the trial got underway that the woman swallowed the phone intentionally to keep the defendant from seeing whom she had been calling.

Source: The Associated Press

A Tempe, Arizona police officer demanded that two black motorists improvise a rap in order to escape a ticket for throwing trash out of their car window. The two nervously managed to do so, and the whole incident was recorded on videotape. Local community leaders said that the tape illustrates the need for better police diversity training.

Source: The Week

Searches for accommodations in Kazakhstan on hotels.com have jumped by 300 percent since the release of the movie

Borat: Cultural Learnings of America for Make Benefit Glorious Nation of Kazakhstan.

Source: The Wall Street Journal

A Massachusetts man was fired after his urine tested positive for nicotine. Scott Rodriguez, 30, was dismissed by Scotts Company, the lawn care specialists, under a new policy that forbids workers from using tobacco.

Source: The Week

A female passenger on an American Airlines flight had an episode of flatulence and lit several matches to hide the smell. Alarmed fellow passengers reported a sharp burning odor, and the flight made an emergency landing in Nashville, where all 99 passengers were searched and interrogated by the FBI.

Source: The Week

Foreigners hold a record 52 percent of the US government's $4 trillion in outside debt, up from 25 percent in 1995.

Source: USA Today

Actor James Barbour, who played the Beast in the Broadway production of *Beauty and the Beast*, was charged with sexually molesting a 15-year-old female fan who came backstage to express her admiration.

Source: The Week

Though outlawed throughout the world, slavery has made a disturbing comeback. The slave trade is now the third largest type of illegal trade in the world, after drugs and weapons.

Source: U.S. State Department

The brand name Häagen-Dazs was thought up during a 1959 brainstorming session between Rose Mattus and her husband, Reuben, a Bronx couple who created America's first luxury-brand ice cream. With visions of Danish milkmaids ladling out cream, an inspired Reuben tossed out a nonsense name that, to his ears, sounded perfectly Danish. To make it seem more authentic, Reuben added an umlaut (ä), which isn't even used in the Danish language.

Source: The London Independent

Inertia

March 7, 2007

INERTIA IS A strong force indeed.
In 1975 I was all of 14, and spending a lot of time away from my native Colombia and in South Florida, totally awestruck by the wonder that was (and is) the United States. And dreaming of someday living here permanently (a dream that came true just three years later) . . . but I digress.

GM's catchy slogan for its 1975 vision of "a new kind of American car" in the face of the Arab oil embargo of 1973 is one of my sharpest memories of that year. If you are old enough to have been horrified by *The Exorcist* in an actual movie theater, you may even remember the entire jingle:

> It's about time
> it's about time
> it's about time
> for a new kind of American car.
>
> It's about time for a new kind of car
> and we've got it.

> Chevette is a new kind
> of American car.

Yes, the astonishingly pathetic Chevette. Shortly followed by Ford's "new kind of American car," the "hit me from behind and I'll actually explode" Pinto. Little did I know it at the time, but with hindsight I now realize that Chevette and Pinto marked the beginning of the end of the U.S auto industry's dominance of the domestic car market. It took Toyota over 30 years to surpass Ford and become the world's #2 automaker (it will probably pass GM to become #1 in a year or two), but the stage was, no doubt, set in the mid-seventies. Detroit's lackluster reaction to the end of cheap gasoline, its refusal to make the severe changes necessary to adapt to a drastically changing marketplace, and the emergence of high-quality, low-cost automobiles from Japan brought it decades of steady decline. Today, the combined U.S. market share for Chrysler, Ford and General Motors is an unbelievably sad 53 percent (source: Edmunds.com), and we are not even addressing the fact that Chrysler is now part of DaimlerChrysler, and thus arguably no longer a U.S. carmaker.

(The following may seem totally unrelated to the foregoing, but please bear with me.)

The oft-delayed, once-renamed Windows Vista was released to consumers in January 2007. And although Vista sports many significant improvements over its predecessor, Windows XP, particularly in the security area, it is by no means a revolutionary product. It is not even what I would call a vast improvement over XP. One could actually argue, without risk of ridicule, that each of Mac OS X's versions—10.1 ("Puma"), 10.2 ("Jaguar"), 10.3 ("Panther"), 10.4 ("Tiger"), and the upcoming 10.5 ("Leopard")—probably represented more of an improvement over its immediate predecessor than Vista does over XP.

And the upgrade process to all of Mac OS X's new versions has been straightforward and relatively painless, in absolute contrast to Vista, for which the best upgrade advise is: don't. Buy a new PC with Vista pre-installed instead. And even if you do purchase a brand-new Vista PC, you will be annoyed by all sorts of evidence of a not-fully-baked product. Apple, in hilarious good nature, pokes fun at Vista's new User Account Control (UAC) mechanism, likening it to an omnipresent security agent, irritatingly asking for approval for mundane, everyday tasks. Even Jim Louderback, editor of *PC* magazine (for crying out loud), is frustrated by Vista's "haphazard" wireless networking, "inadequate" driver support, terrible "sleep" implementation and inconsistent VPN support. And Louderback is an unabashed Windows guy!

So, you ask, what does Vista have to do with Chevette? I think Vista marks the beginning of the end of Windows' dominant market share of the world's desktop computers. Throughout its history, Windows has never really been anything but a mediocre implementation of others' ideas. But Microsoft's business and marketing prowess gave rise to Windows' eventual ubiquity. And, for many years thereafter, there were simply no feasible alternatives to Windows, as the aging original Mac OS became less compatible with the rest of the world and more of a niche product, and no other operating systems appeared on the scene. But all that has changed, and how!

Mac OS X is an elegant, robust system, fully integrated with the hardware it runs on, providing an unparalleled user experience. And the ubiquity of TCP/IP and the Web has made it an equal player when it comes to networking, browsing and email. Mac OS X's thriving developer community constantly brings all sorts of cool applications to the platform. Today, Mac OS X can seamlessly coexist with Windows, besting it at almost everything. Linux has come of age as a formidable server OS, and as such runs a significant percentage of the world's Web servers. It has also gained some traction on the desktop, particularly in international markets. Web-based applications are finally delivering on their long-ago promises, evidenced by services such as those offered by Google, NetSuite, Salesforce.com, 37Signals, and a host of others. As these services become more prevalent, compatibility becomes universal and people are suddenly free to choose the operating system they would like to use, as opposed to being forced to use the one that runs their applications.

So the stage is set. Vista is the Chevette of 2007. Not due to similarities in the products themselves; Vista may have its shortcomings, but it would be a tad unfair to liken it to the hapless Chevette. No, the similarities lie in each product's overarching significance to their manufacturer's future. A spectacular Vista could have cemented Windows dominance for decades to come, just as a spectacular Chevette could have done the same for the U.S. auto industry. Alas, the lame Chevette was the harbinger of the decline of the U.S. auto industry. Likewise, the underwhelming Vista is the harbinger of the end of Windows' dominance of the world's desktops. Mac OS X and Linux represent the up-and-coming players in the marketplace, as the Japanese carmakers did in the mid-seventies. And (you heard it here first, folks), these factors will combine to reduce Windows' share of the worldwide desktop market to below 50 percent in five years. That's right, we are boldly predicting, here and now, that by the spring of 2012 half of the world's computers will run operating systems other than Windows.

"It's about time for a new kind of American car" (Chevette)

"Wow" (Vista)

Two slogans. Two products. Two industries. In both cases, the beginning of the end.

GrandCentral

March 24, 2007

GRANDCENTRAL IS AN amazing idea whose time has come. Or, GrandCentral is an amazing idea whose time has passed.

GrandCentral is a free Web service available at www.grandcentral.com. You sign up and obtain a new phone number (many of the most popular area codes in the U.S. are available). And that single phone number can easily become the last number you'll ever need. Because you are in complete control of what happens when anyone calls that number. You can set it to ring at your home. You can set it to ring at your office. You can set it to ring on your cell phone. You can set it to ring at all three at the same time, and choose which one to answer. Astonishingly, you can even transfer calls from one phone to another on the fly. For instance, if you set your GrandCentral phone number to ring your cell phone and your office phone, and you take a call on your cell phone while in your car, upon arrival to your office you can transfer the call to your office phone while the call is in progress! The person on the other end of the call will not even notice.

Of course, if you decide not to take the call, GrandCentral will take a voice message. Here again, you are in complete control. You can listen to your voicemail by calling in from any telephone. You can also access your voicemail by logging into GrandCentral's Web site. You can set GrandCentral to email you your voice messages. And, hold on here, folks, you can actually listen in while your caller leaves you the voicemail, and decide at any time to take the call, like you do with your home answering machine!

Oh, and there's more. You can set up different greetings for different callers. As many different callers as you want. You can even change the phone "ring" that your callers listen to before either you or the greeting picks up to any sound; maybe a song you like, or background noise, or whatever you can put into MP3 format and upload to GrandCentral's Web site.

GrandCentral represents the end of checking multiple voicemail repositories. The end of telling people, "I'll be at my home phone for a couple of hours, after that you can reach me on my cell." The end of taking calls you didn't really want to take. The end of missing phone calls. GrandCentral is, essentially, the perfect voice communications system. And yes, it's free, as long as you only have two numbers to consolidate and you don't mind seeing ads on the Web site. For $15 per month you get to consolidate up to six numbers, and enjoy an ad-free Web site.

So, GrandCentral is an amazing idea whose time has come, right? Well, I was so impressed by GrandCentral when I first came across it a few months ago that I immediately signed up. However, I haven't used my GrandCentral account at all. Why? Consider this: my cell phone is constantly in my pocket. At work, home, while traveling, wherever. Anyone who knows me knows that the way to reach me is on my cell phone, and everyone who knows me has that number. My office phone is set to automatically forward calls to my cell phone if it is not answered in two rings. My cell phone works in almost every country on the planet. If I decide to change cell carrier (as I have done in the past), I take my number with me. The only voicemail I check is the one on my cell phone.

So GrandCentral solves a problem that I already solved with my cell phone. And many others have done the same. And the generation now coming into adulthood understands communications in what we will call the "Star Trek" style: one person, one communications device, one number. Will they ever need a service like GrandCentral? I think not. I think they will use their "personal communicator" (today a cell phone, tomorrow perhaps a VoIP system, using what I'm sure will be ubiquitous wireless Internet access) regardless of where they are. Home landlines, and even home-based VoIP systems will become a thing of the past. Office switchboards will also disappear, as people take (or ignore) calls and use voicemail on their personal devices, and transfer calls to powerful speaker devices (or video conferencing systems) when needed. Just like *Star Trek*. One person, one number. No need to consolidate telephone numbers.

So, is GrandCentral an amazing idea whose time has come, or an amazing idea whose time has passed? Only time will tell.

Sports and the Holocaust

March 28, 2007

IF YOU FIND it difficult to believe that human beings were capable of carrying out as grotesque an endeavor as the Nazi Holocaust, you will be easily convinced if you attend certain sporting events. For the same callous disregard for others, us-versus-them mentality, and astonishing abandonment of any sort of objective thought that made the "Final Solution" even fathomable to the Nazis is on display when passion tramples reason at stadiums and arenas all over the world.

During last weekend's "friendly" soccer match between Colombia and Switzerland at Miami's venerable Orange Bowl, for example, the heavily partisan Colombian crowd erupted into hearty chants of "son of a whore" toward the referees every time an even slightly questionable call went against their team. Hard fouls by Colombian players, even when they resulted in injury to an opponent, were roundly applauded. There was no sense of enjoying a hard-fought contest between teams of talented athletes. The fans' only interest was in their team's victory; sportsmanship, indeed humanity, be damned. Ironically, the players on the historic Orange Bowl turf constantly displayed exemplary behavior and sportsmanship, always hastening to help an opponent up after a foul, or patting them on the back after an unintentional hit. Bewilderingly, these acts of gentlemanliness and good manners (which warmed my heart much more than any of my native Colombia's goals that afternoon) were entirely lost on the spectators, who would have done well to follow the players' examples. I am decidedly proud of my Colombian origin and ethnicity, but that afternoon I felt thoroughly embarrassed by my countrymen's behavior. For crying out loud, this was a meaningless "friendly" match!

But the disconcerting behavior of the fans at the Orange Bowl last weekend pales in comparison to that of followers of Argentina's River Plate soccer club during an important club tournament match against Colombia's America team in 1996. My wife and I happened to attend the match, held at Buenos Aires' so-called Monumental Stadium. While on our way to the game, our hosts advised us not to disclose my national origin lest our safety be jeopardized. Naively, I thought they were kidding. It didn't take long, once we were in the unfriendly confines of the stadium, which, by the way, is everything but "monumental," for us to realize that, hey, they weren't kidding. For the following two hours, the athletes of Colombia's America were abused in every possible way a human being can be abused from a distance. Hideous insults, all sorts of debris thrown on the field (even when the ball was in play), clearly demonstrated the fans' shocking lack of respect for their fellow human beings. It is difficult in the extreme to confuse me with a prude, but some of the language I heard that night deeply offended me. There was absolutely no sense of fair play; the fans' only objectives were to give River Plate an unfair advantage and disgustingly wallow in their victory. After the game was mercifully over (River Plate won, 3–1), River Plate's players actually stripped down to their jockstraps on the field and paraded themselves about, in a crude display that can only be described as an appalling orgy of inappropriateness.

It is obviously unfair to single out the Colombian partisans at the Orange Bowl or the River Plate faithful; I simply use them as examples because of the lasting impression those two particular experiences made on me. The Orange Bowl experience hurt me much more; apparently it feels better to be associated with the victims of abuse than with its perpetrators. To a lesser extent, I have personally experienced similar attitudes at Ohio State University and University of Miami college football games. Sadly, violence at sporting events is commonplace everywhere. Of course, I have also experienced the joy of watching well-played athletic contests where the fans support their team but never lose perspective; indeed some of my most pleasurable moments related to sports have involved moments of greatness by athletes that transcended any kind of partisanship. When Michael Jordan amazed the crowds with his spellbinding talent at the Miami Arena during the '90s, the crowd put their team affiliation to one side, understanding that they were in the midst of greatness. But, no matter what talents could have been displayed by an America player that 1996 night in Buenos Aires, the fans would have surely derided the display in a heap of shortsighted negativity.

You may question the perhaps extreme comparison between rude sports fans and Nazis. However, I have absolutely no doubt that if an America player would have in any way injured a River Plate player, even unintentionally, during the 1996 game I witnessed, and the fans had been allowed on the field, the America player would have been pummeled to death in a matter of minutes by the frenzied River Plate faithful. Common decency, regard for others, and indeed basic humanity are easily cast aside when passion overwhelms, and everyday frustrations are channeled and vented in the form of hate. The America players in Buenos Aires and the Swiss players at the Orange Bowl became symbols of everything wrong with the lives of the fans, and, as symbols, they were no longer considered human beings. And it's easy to abuse a symbol, especially when everyone around you is doing the same. Parallels to the Nazi Holocaust are palpably evident.

"If passion drives, let reason hold the reins," said Benjamin Franklin. Given how easy it is for us to be driven by runaway passion while pushing reason away, it is not surprising in the least that the Holocaust happened. What's surprising is that it hasn't happened more often.

Official Scorer

April 29, 2007

THE GAME OF baseball is beautiful in many ways, perhaps none more so than the symmetry and relentless pursuit of fairness in its statistics. More than any other endeavor, baseball attempts to faithfully account for everything that happens on the field and assign credit and blame in a just, objective manner. If you have experienced the joy of keeping score at a baseball game, you know that, at the end of the day, your scorecard tells the story of the contest with a degree of completeness and attribution unique to baseball.

If you are among those of us who have delighted in scoring a baseball game, no further explanation is necessary. However, if you count yourself among those deprived souls who have never taken pencil to lap-perched, beer-stained scorecard, here's some background. A baseball scorecard consists of a grid with each inning represented by a vertical column and each player listed on a horizontal row. Each square on the grid, then, represents one plate appearance. And the entire pitch-by-pitch account of each appearance is faithfully recorded within its appropriate square, using a unique shorthand of abbreviations and diagrams. Therefore, a quick glance at the scorecard will tell you, for example, that Bobby Murcer, the Yankee's center fielder*, struck out in the first inning, hit a 3-1 pitch to right-center field for a double in the third inning (and scored when the batter that followed him got a base hit), flied out to center field in the sixth, reached first base on an error by the shortstop in the ninth, and was thrown out attempting to steal second.

At this point you may be scratching your head, thinking, how can everyone's scorecards match up? Certainly, many plays may be scored differently depending on the scorer's opinion. For example, one spectator may feel that the ground ball mishandled by the shortstop in the ninth inning of our Murcer example was simply a base hit, since the infielder did not have a reasonable chance of handling it cleanly. Another spectator, perhaps sitting right next to the first one, may feel that the infielder

---

*There is a bit of significance to my choice of Murcer, of all people, as an example. Growing up in soccer-crazed Colombia, my introduction to baseball came relatively late in life, at summer camp in upstate New York in 1972. At Camp Lenni-Len-A-Pe, an integral part of our daily flag-raising routine was the announcement of the previous night's baseball scores and highlights by one of the older campers, whose name sadly escapes me, but whose voice I can almost hear as I write this. Murcer, as the Yankee's star center fielder, was frequently mentioned at those early-morning announcements and thus became the first baseball player I ever knew by name. Murcer went on to have a solid career, but never lived up to the initial expectations unfairly assigned to him, having had the misfortune of following Joe DiMaggio and fellow Oklahoman Mickey Mantle at center field for the Yankees. Murcer moved from the diamond to the broadcast booth, and continued broadcasting Yankee games on TV and radio until late last year, when he was diagnosed with a brain tumor on Christmas Eve. He underwent surgery on December 28th, and is presently in recovery. Murcer received a rousing standing ovation during an appearance at Yankee Stadium on opening day earlier this month.

made an error; that the play was not a base hit. And each one of them will record the play on their scorecard differently, right?

Actually, no. Everyone will record the play exactly the same way, regardless of their personal opinion. Because baseball, in its infinite wisdom, provides for an "Official Scorer"; a person at the ballpark who keeps, you guessed it, the official score. If the Official Scorer scores the play an error, that is what it is. Period. You may agree or disagree (and sometimes millions of dollars are at stake, since players' contracts contain high-value incentive clauses based on statistics) but regardless of what you think, you record the play on your scorecard as the Official Scorer does on his, for that is the definitive word.

Obviously the Official Scorer is not the only person making judgment calls at a baseball game. Four (or sometimes even more) umpires are on the field, determining whether each pitch is a ball or a strike, whether a base runner was beaten by the throw, whether a ball is fair or foul, and so on. However, the umpires are charged with objective judgments based on fact. The Official Scorer gets to decide on matters of subjective judgment—matters where the rule book is of no help. Was that a wild pitch or a passed ball? Should the outfielder have caught that line drive? Was that throw to first base simply too high, or did the first baseman have a reasonable shot at catching it? Simply put, the umpires determine what happened. The Official Scorer determines what should have happened.

So, at the end of the game, your scorecard tells you that the aforementioned Murcer had four plate appearances and got on base twice. The kind of information available from the stat sheet of any sport. But your scorecard goes on to tell you that Murcer really shouldn't have gotten on base that second time, and only did so because the shortstop muffed his ground ball in the ninth. So we know what happened, but we also know what should have happened. Murcer should have been out. And the statistics will reflect that: he will not get a hit, and his batting average will suffer for it.

And that seemingly minor nuance differentiates baseball from all other sports. For baseball is the only one that earnestly attempts to do the right thing. Every time. No matter what.

If only life were that way!

> **Update**
>
> From the Wikipedia article on Bobby Murcer (http://en.wikipedia.org/wiki/Bobby_Murcer): "In late February, 2008, a magnetic resonance imaging (MRI) caused Murcer's doctors to do a biopsy. On March 5, 2008, Murcer received good news: that the biopsy revealed scar tissue, rather than a recurrence of brain cancer. Murcer stated he planned to rest until spring training where he plans to call Yankee games and work in the YES Network studio."

We Have Lost the War

June 1, 2007

WE HAVE LOST the war on terrorism. We cannot board an airplane without first being subjected to insanely long security checkpoint queues, ineffective yet painfully intrusive searches, inane rules regarding shoes, laptops, liquids, 3-ounce containers, and Ziploc bags (3-1-1, anyone?), and, in general, an air travel security policy that eschews effective yet possibly politically incorrect strategies to instead insult, annoy, violate, and humiliate all of us equally. I challenge the TSA to produce one, just one, potentially explosive liquid among the millions of tons of innocuous materials confiscated from innocent travelers. Moreover, I challenge the TSA to produce evidence of one, just one, terrorist act thwarted by airport security. When terrorists have been caught, as in London last year, it has been through solid intelligence and old-fashioned police work. Not by depriving old ladies of their toothpaste.

Our air travel security policy is disturbingly onerous, yet pathetically ineffective.

We have lost the war on credit card fraud.

We cannot make a couple of credit card purchases outside of our normal routine one day without that very evening being subjected to a grilling by a patronizing, polite-to-the-point-of-annoyance gentleman from Mumbai. Yet hundreds of cases of identity theft occur every month, and millions of dollars are lost—and gained, of course, by the thieves.

Credit card companies are at least three steps behind the scammers.

We have lost the war on spam.

It is conservatively estimated that over 90 percent of all email is spam. We cannot open our inboxes without being subjected to countless offers to extravagantly enhance our manhood, or amazingly be singled out to participate in once-in-a-lifetime stock opportunities. We therefore have no choice but to implement flawed tools to combat spam, which partially resolve the issue yet sadly bring on countless problems of their own.

Our primary communication system is actually abused more than it is used.

We have lost the war on hackers.

It is estimated that over 30 percent of all Windows-based personal computers are, in fact, zombies constantly spewing spam at the behest of their overlords, totally unbeknownst to their hapless owners, who pathetically wonder why their PCs seem to be "acting so sluggishly lately." These days we cannot run our computers without first establishing complex security schemes involving firewalls, anti-virus software and anti-spyware software (unless, of course, we run Macs). We cannot surf the Web without running the risk of nefarious Web sites running all sorts of malicious scripts on our machines. We cannot assume that an email seemingly from our bank is in fact from our bank, but have to assume that it is from some malevolent hacker.

The most important device that we own is, quite possibly, co-owned by some Russian zombie tycoon.

Alas, humanity is like one giant cancer patient, with some of its cells inexplicably turning against the whole. And those in charge, like hapless doctors, are both unable to determine the cause of the turncoat cells' behavior and impotent against their actions. So they resort to punishing the whole, hoping that the good will not be washed away with the bad. The patient is weak, dear reader, with no signs of remission.

On Faith

June 17, 2007

FAITH, FOR THE purposes of this essay, is defined as "a strong belief in God or in the doctrines of a religion, based on spiritual apprehension rather than proof." My view is that people of faith fall into five categories:

1. The "Shysters," or people who don't actually believe themselves, yet preach a phony faith to sincere believers for fun and profit. You may toss the Jim Bakkers and Jimmy Swaggarts of the world into this category, as well as countless others who have not yet been exposed as frauds.
2. The "Stockholm Syndromers." (Please refer to "We're All In Stockholm" on page 85 for a definition of Stockholm Syndrome.) In this context, the individual reaches out to the most powerful force they perceive to be available to them in times of danger, namely God. Faith through fear, quite possibly the most populous faith category.
3. The "Sinners," or people who believe they can get away with evildoing as long as they somehow braid their wick-

edness with strands of grotesquely passionate belief, oblivious to the 800-pound contradiction between the teachings of their chosen religion and their actual deeds. Classic examples of Sinners abound in *The Godfather* and other mobster movies, but you can easily spot them yourself at your friendly neighborhood place of worship.

4. The "Great Pretenders." No, not The Platters (although they may or may not have faith), but those who don't really believe in God, and privately question his (or hers, or its?) existence, but follow along just because it's the path of least resistance. Somehow, among our society's mores, we have built this astonishingly irrational notion that belief in God is nice, and good, and non-belief is somehow evil (more on this later). Hogwash, of course, but try telling that to one who has been "born again"! The "Great Pretenders" sadly pretend to have faith simply not to make waves.

5. The "Sinceres," or people who frankly, honestly, and sincerely believe in a Superior Being of some sort, or a "higher energy," or a "light," or something. They may not understand the details; they may not have all the answers, but nonetheless, they are certain about their beliefs, which are pure and devoid of ulterior motives or fear. The people in this sparsely populated group, regardless of their adherence (or not) to any form of organized religion, are the only true "faithful."

If you are a frequent Sifter Stickers reader (and if you are, thank you for reading!), or if you happen to know me personally, you also know that it is difficult to confuse me with a man of faith. I believe in what makes sense to me, and if I can't make sense of it, I simply acknowledge that I don't know the answer. I respect people of all faiths, and I respect the faiths of all peoples. I, quite simply, don't have faith, don't need it, and (gasp!) am able to live a happy and productive life without it. I believe in what I can understand, and cheerfully file things that I cannot yet understand into a folder not surprisingly labeled "things I don't yet understand."

People of faith do many things that I find irrational, and to delve into these things and why I find them irrational is way beyond the scope of this particular essay. Here, I simply would like to briefly focus on one of the acts I find to be most irrational, as well as highly destructive. People of faith, as well as people in groups 1–4 above, tend to believe that their own belief system is somehow superior to that of others. Furthermore, as much as they believe that people who have faith in a different construct than they do are somehow incorrect or misguided, they tend to believe that, well, at least they have faith, which is to say that there is nothing worse than having no faith at all.

Now let's understand this properly. I have an irrational belief in something for which there is absolutely no evidence, but against which there is plenty of evidence. Yet I feel that those who believe in other, equally irrational doctrines, are somehow deluded. And I feel that those who don't believe in any irrational doctrine but simply admit that the answers to certain questions lie beyond their understanding at this time are, bless their pathetic souls, totally lost.

OK, dear reader, the metaphor that comes to mind is this: You have a few too many shots of the Cuervo Gold, or a few too many tokes on the Fine Colombian (which, with a nod to Steely Dan, make tonight a wonderful thing). You see pink elephants dancing on your stovetop. And you believe that those around you who see blue giraffes are just not understanding reality, man. And those who just see a plain stovetop, well, they just haven't hit their groove, man.

Except there is no Cuervo. And no Colombian, Fine or otherwise. And yet you still see the elephants. And you still feel the same way about those who don't.

eBay

June 24, 2007

SO A CLIENT asked me to sell an old PowerBook for her on eBay.
Now, I'm not exactly an eBay maven, but I have sold a computer or two, a couple of sporting event tickets, and a few other items on the auction site, and I do have 100 percent positive feedback, so I was happy to set up a seven-day auction for the PowerBook, even though I hadn't actually used eBay for a few months.

Once the item was posted, the following week brought 15 questions from potential buyers; normally an encouraging sign. Alas, only three of the questions were actually bona fide, asking if the original CDs and packing materials were included with the Mac, or if the optical drive was able to burn DVDs. The other 12 questions? Well, two of them were not really questions, but offers to sell me all kinds of amazing electronic products at astonishingly low prices. The remaining ten "questions" are best exemplified by the one I received from eBay member "mehannah," copied verbatim below:

Dear Seller,

I'm Mrs Loore Moore from USA.I'm highly interested in purchasing your item placed on EBAY for my only son that study in Nigeria as a birthday gift.I will offer you the sum of Euro 1,800 for these item + shipping through (Fedex express 3-5 Days Delivery) to Nigeria due to it urgent need,and i will like to know if you have more items for sale so that it will be offered once.Payment will be made through Royal Bank of Canada Online Wire Transfer Department(Cash Payment).I want you to reply me with your personal E-mail for further conversation via:-(loore_moore@yahoo.com) you can also add me toyour hotmail messager (mrs.love11@hotmail.com)

Kindly provide me your bank details for the payment to be made through Royal bank Of Canada as soon as possible.

Thanks.

Great, the familiar Nigerian scams have branched out into eBay auctions, I sourly thought to myself as I duly reported the inappropriate message as well as the 11 others. A nuisance, to be sure, but hey, what can you do? The auction continued.

On the morning of the seventh and last day of the auction, I felt pretty good about the situation. The leading bid was close to $600, a fair price for the PowerBook, given its age and the price of the new MacBook Pros on the market. I thought we were pretty much home free. Then, of course, disaster struck.

A few minutes before the auction was scheduled to end, a bid for $6,864 was entered. Yes, over ten times the approximate fair value of the computer. The bid obviously won the auction, and I received notice from eBay that my item had sold for $6,864, and that the next step was for me to send the buyer an invoice. I sent the invoice, knowing full well that the chances of the sale being consummated were roughly like the chances of spotting Senator John Edwards at your local Supercuts. About an hour later I received the dismal official notice from eBay that the winner of my auction was, in fact, an account that had been recently hijacked, and eBay was working with the real owner of the account to rectify matters. My sale was, of course, cancelled, since eBay auction runners-up, unlike their beauty pageant brethren, are sadly not called into action should the winner be unable to fulfill her duties and obligations. I was effectively in the middle of downtown Square One city.

A seller, willing to part with an item at a price a buyer was willing to pay; both parties brought together by the brilliant execution of a powerful idea. The transaction tragically thwarted. Chalk another one up for the bad guys. No surprise there, Kemo Sabe.

Update

John Edwards, you may remember, was a candidate for the Democratic nomination who was lambasted by his fellow candidates and the media for his $200+ haircuts.

Ratatouille

July 1, 2007

ACCORDING TO JERRY SEINFELD, "There is no such thing as fun for the whole family; there are no massage parlors with ice cream and free jewelry." Great line, to be sure, but, no offense to Jerry, there is in fact such a thing as fun for the whole family, except it is exceedingly precious, and increasingly rare.

As anyone who has had to endure the inane adventures of the cringe-inducing Barney and his dinosaur friends can attest, children's entertainment is often as irritating to adults as it is entertaining to children. And the syrupy purple one is, astonishingly, a cut above those bizarrely repulsive Teletubbies. Truth is, adult-unfriendly children's entertainment abounds, featuring, among many others, such creations as Pokemon, Yu-Gi-Oh, Avatar, and, of course, the Mighty Morphin' Power Rangers, who hold the distinction of starring in the only theatrical movie I have ever abandoned before it ended, surprisingly not to the chagrin of my then four-year-old daughter, who showed wisdom beyond her years that Sunday afternoon when agreeing to leave the theatre in time to prevent her father from yelling embarrassing obscenities in a large auditorium filled with impressionable children and their lawsuit-happy parents . . . but I digress.

Much entertainment that passes for the "family" kind depends almost entirely on the humor found in flatulence, bodily fluids, and strikes to the groin area. Now I'll laugh at farts and guys getting hit in the balls as much as the next guy, and many writers and actors are truly gifted in this area. However, to assume that the only thing that adults and children have in common as far as entertainment is concerned is an appreciation for flying excrement and food fights is insulting to both groups.

Which brings me to *Ratatouille*, the most recent work of the adjective-defying Pixar Animation Studios (recently purchased by the Walt Disney Company).

Ratatouille is a gem. The quality of its animation is such that it would be a pleasure to watch even if there were neither plot nor voices, yet the story is engaging, the characters well developed, and the acting (voice only, of course) superb. As did all Pixar features before it (*Toy Story*, 1995; *A Bug's Life*, 1998; *Toy Story 2*, 1999; *Monsters, Inc.*, 2001; *Finding Nemo*, 2003; *The Incredibles*, 2004; and *Cars*, 2006), *Ratatouille* finds ways of delighting children and engaging their parents while neither patronizing nor embarrassing either group. And it somehow does it without a single fart. And no one gets hit in the balls.

They say that everyone's a comedian, and that happens to be true, since anyone can slip and fall flat on their ass. And that, for reasons best left to psychologists and sociologists to ponder (maybe while watching reruns of Moe, Larry, and Curly in action), is funny. And yes, one does get entertained while watching *Daddy Day Care*, in the same way as one gets full by eating a box of Twinkies. But to enjoy the work of John Lasseter and his crew at Pixar is to enjoy a nicely marbled ribeye, grilled to your exact liking. Or fresh toro, raw over sushi-style rice balls. Or substitute whatever strikes your personal fancy. And, amazingly, in this case the ribeye costs the same as the Twinkies!

iPhone

July 8, 2007

LET'S GET THE negative stuff out of the way first. Apple's amazing new iPhone does not sync to-do items. When not connected to Wi-Fi, it runs on AT&T's pokey EDGE network and not one of the faster 3G networks (at least this first generation iPhone does). And iPhone lacks a Search function, so if you are unsure, say, of a contact's last name you will have a difficult time finding it.

All that said, iPhone's groundbreaking interface, featuring its multi-touch display, is as significant to the development of handheld devices as the mouse was to the development if the personal computer. For although iPhone packs similar functionality to that of my previous handheld, a Blackberry Pearl—or that of my previous-to-that Treo, for that matter—the way in which it performs those familiar functions and seamlessly integrates them places it in a unique category, instantly rendering the aforementioned Blackberries, Treos, and the like hopelessly dated.

It seems that among all electronics manufacturers today, only Apple understands that stuffing features into a product without regard for the user experience does not constitute true innovation. Take the Nokia N95. Please. The N95 is a technological marvel, with a feature list that puts the iPhone's to shame. Yet the Nokia's features sport such a steep learning curve that most users never master them, and even those who do seldom use them because they are such a chore. In stunning contrast, iPhone's deliciously intuitive interface makes it more than just easy, it actually makes it pleasurable to harness its considerable functionality. Manufacturers can always add features; for example, each of the shortcomings I describe in the opening paragraph can and will be addressed by Apple through software and/or firmware updates, or in the case of the G3 network, perhaps a second model. But it's difficult to make a clunky interface elegant through software updates. And the user experience is seldom improved significantly with a new firmware release.

iPhone's interface has absolutely no learning curve. Everything just works as you expect it will, and looks absolutely gorgeous in the process. And the seamless integration among functions is elegantly efficient. iPhone does so many things so well and so easily that it may become, perhaps in a future generation, the handheld device that finally makes traveling with a laptop obsolete.

Time will tell if iPhone will eventually go the way of the Mac, a clearly superior product with an inexplicably low market share, or the way of the iPod, dominating its market as it clearly deserves to based on its advanced interface.

My money's on the latter.

TWREoHID IV

August 5, 2007

THIS WEEK'S RANDOM evidence of humanity's impending downfall (Volume 4):

A Pasadena, California online magazine last week hired two reporters to cover the local government who have never set foot in Pasadena, and probably never will. In fact, they are half a world away, in Mumbai and Bangalore, India. PasadenaNow.com publisher James MacPherson explains that Pasadena City Council meetings are webcast, so his far-flung reporters can observe the proceedings over the Internet and file stories electronically.

Source: The Week

Carey McWilliams, 33, has permits from North Dakota and Utah to carry concealed weapons, despite the fact that he is legally blind.

Source: buzzle.com

Last week a German couple had to call the fire department after chaining each other up during their first-ever bondage session and losing the key to the padlock.

Source: The Week

An Illinois woman who fell and broke her ankle while attempting to dance on the top of a bar is suing the establishment for not stopping her. Amy Mueller wants more than $50,000 from the owners of Samy's Bar and Grill for "allowing [her] to climb upon the bar without a step stool, ladder or other device used for safety," according to her lawsuit.

Source: The Chicago Tribune

Princess Martha Louise of Norway announced to the world that she has been communicating directly with angels since childhood.

Source: The Sydney Morning Herald

A Middle Eastern businessman and 17 guests racked up a $200,000 bar bill at a London nightclub.

Source: The Week

A New Hampshire Republican organization has announced a fundraiser at which party members and their families can fire Uzi submachine guns, M-16 rifles, and other military-style weapons. Organizer Jerry Thibodeau of Manchester said the $25 entrance fee would entitle attendees to fire weapons they might never otherwise get to handle, while simultaneously supporting the right to bear arms. "It's a fun day. It's a family day," said Thibodeau.

Source: Reuters

A Florida man was charged with misusing 911 after he called the emergency number to report that he was surrounded by policemen. Responding to earlier reports of a disturbance in a bar, police in Largo, Florida found Dana Shelton, 28, in a state of apparent intoxication. Shelton then pulled out his cell phone, dialed 911, slurred to the dispatcher that he was "surrounded by Largo policemen," and asked her to send help. "Our officers were standing there scratching their heads," said Sgt. Melanie Holley.

Source: The Canadian Press

Rock star Sting arrived at a top Miami restaurant with his personal chef, who cooked a one-person meal for him in the restaurant's kitchen. Italian eatery Casa Tua is known for the quality of its food as much as its celebrity clientele, but Sting, 55, a health enthusiast, was only interested in food prepared to his own specifications. "His people booked ahead and said the staff could cook for his friends but not for him," a witness said.

Source: The London Sun

Shades of the Same Hue

August 26, 2007

He was born on June 26, 1980 in Newport News, Virginia into financially disadvantaged circumstances, and grew up in a public housing project. Yet he became a standout high school football player and attended Virginia Tech University on a full scholarship. After two successful seasons as a Hokie, he opted to enter the NFL draft, and was selected by the Atlanta Falcons as their first overall pick. He quickly became one of the highest-paid NFL players, and earned various lucrative commercial product endorsements.

He was widely seen as a role model and success story.

In July 2007 he was charged by federal authorities, along with three others, on felony charges of operating an unlawful six-year-long interstate dog fighting venture at his property in Surry County, Virginia. After initially adamantly denying any role in the dog fighting operation, he admitted bankrolling the entire enterprise, and personally participating in the tortuous killing of dogs "not worthy of the pit."

He agreed to a plea bargain on August 20th, and is expected to receive a federal prison sentence between 12 months and 5 years. He may also face state charges in Virginia.

NFL Commissioner Roger Goodell indefinitely suspended him without pay.

His endorsement deals are, for all practical purposes, nothing but fond memories.

Donruss and Upper Deck, trading card companies, pulled his card from future releases.

He may never play professional football again.

As much as we enjoy rags-to-riches stories, we seem to enjoy riches-to-rags stories even more. Michael Vick was not widely known outside of the world of the NFL when he was a shining example of all that is good: a poor, disadvantaged boy rises to the top of the professional sports world on the wings of his talent. But the irrevocably tarnished Vick's fame now easily transcends professional sports. Good news, of course, attracts nowhere near the eyeballs that a good horror story does.

Michael Vick is the man we love to hate today. He's an easy target, the perfect poster boy. Many will say, of course, that he grew up with violence, that it's part of who he is. Many will use the fact that Vick was poor growing up to distance themselves from him and his deplorable actions. And, of course, there are those who will absurdly yet predictably bring the fact that Michael Vick is black into the equation, further separating themselves from him. But they will be fooling themselves, for the attraction to violence among humans knows no boundaries and is in no way related to race, class, ethnicity or financial status.

Many Spaniards and Latin Americans enjoy bullfights, during which a defenseless animal is relentlessly taunted, gored, punctured, and ridiculed before finally being stabbed to death, often hacked multiple times before the matador (literally, "killer") achieves the fatal plunge of the sword. The British have their fox hunts (also practiced in the U.S., Canada, New Zealand, Australia, and India), where trained dogs and human hunters pursue and kill red foxes. Well-established cockfighting arenas exist in Nicaragua, Belgium, Colombia, France, Mexico, Dominican Republic, Italy, Philippines, Peru, Puerto Rico, the Canary Islands, and Guam, and while cockfighting is today considered a form of animal cruelty in the United States, it was once considered to be a traditional sporting event. And, of course, we have the dog fight, which originated in Japan and is widely practiced in Afghanistan, Argentina, Colombia, many parts of Brazil, Russia, and the United Kingdom. Although dog fighting is illegal in all North American countries, it is still commonly practiced, particularly by gangs.

And yes, many of us are repulsed by dog fights, bullfights, fox hunts and cockfights. But animal abuse is but one of many forms of violence enjoyed by human spectators. Boxing and wrestling (with varying degrees of realism) are popular in many parts of the world (including, of course, the United States). And many contact sports, particularly ice hockey, American football, and rugby, are inherently violent. George Orwell once made the observation, "Serious sport has nothing to do with fair play. It is bound up with hatred, jealousy, boastfulness, disregard of all rules and sadistic pleasure in witnessing violence: in other words it is war minus the shooting." And, lest we forget, we must mention violent movies, TV shows, and video games, cornerstones of the entertainment industry.

So we can look at Michael Vick with smug repulsion, in utter disbelief of his incomprehensible attraction to bloody violence. We can use irrelevant superficialities such as his background and race to distance ourselves from him. We can point to him and say that he is clearly everything we are not. But in doing so we would be sadly mistaken, for taken in the context of human history, Michael Vick's cruelty and disdain for fellow living creatures is, tragically, not the aberrant behavior we would like it to be but instead an extreme expression of the ugliness that lies within all of us.

After all, Michael Vick enjoying a gruesome dog fight, fans applauding a vicious hit on the football field, and a kid (perhaps mine, or yours) enjoying a game of Grand Theft Auto represent different shades of the same putrid hue.

> **Update**
>
> From the Wikipedia page about Michael Vick (http://en.wikipedia.org/wiki/Michael_Vick): "In 2007, a U.S. federal district court convicted Vick and several co-defendants of criminal conspiracy resulting from felonious dog fighting and lying and sentenced him to serve a 23-month prison sentence. He is being held in the United States Penitentiary at Leavenworth, Kansas."

Anticipation

September 3, 2007

ALTHOUGH PITTSBURGH NATIVE Oscar Levant (1906–1972) was a pianist and composer, he was better known for his mordant character and witticisms than for his music. Among some of his more biting remarks:

"Roses are red, violets are blue, I am schizophrenic, and so am I."

"What the world needs is more geniuses with humility, there are so few of us left."

"I'm a concert pianist—that's a pretentious way of saying I'm unemployed at the moment."

"Everyone in Hollywood is gay, except Gabby Hayes—and that's because he is a transvestite."

In a rare moment of forthrightness, Levant remarked, "Happiness is not something you experience, it's something you remember." Not as witty, perhaps, or as controversial as most of his repartee, but insightful nonetheless, since we seem to habitually take our happiness for granted—until we no longer have it.

Today I enjoyed an afternoon baseball game with my nine-year-old son, Isaac. We sat at the facility that should be known as Joe Robbie Stadium, drenched with South Florida's glorious late summer sunshine, as our beloved last-place Marlins came back from a 5–0 deficit to lead 7–5 at the top of the ninth, then almost blew the lead before hanging on to beat the playoff-contending Philadelphia Phillies 7–6 in an absolute blast of a game. And while Isaac and I discussed baseball's subtle nuances, and I reflected on other aspects of my life, the exquisite Carly Simon provided the perfect background soundtrack for the scene, as her 1971 classic "Anticipation" played over the stadium's PA system, seemingly for my own listening pleasure. For although, sadly, it became impossible for an entire generation to hear this gorgeous song without thinking of ketchup pouring slowly out of a bottle, I've always marveled at its inspired lyrics, in particular its last line, which rang clear and true today, just as it has for the past few years: " . . . these are the good old days."

For I realize now that in years to come I will look back at these as the best times of my life. And although our tendency is, as Levant observed, not to experience today's happiness but instead to remember it tomorrow, when perhaps it is no longer around, we can dare to defy the witty Pittsburgher. For it is possible to have it both ways; to actually experience happiness in real time and still fondly remember it later. Carly had it right in '71, when she expressed in just a few words what so-called self-help advocates attempt to convey in lengthy tomes and expensive seminars. Stop "chasing after some finer day" and "stay right here, 'cause these are the good old days."

Transcend Attachments
September 19, 2007

"ATTACHMENT LEADS TO jealousy. The shadow of greed, that is. Train yourself to let go . . . of everything you fear to lose."

Unfortunately, Master Yoda's words fell on deaf ears. When the time came for young Jedi Anakin Skywalker to choose between good and evil, with no less than the fate of the galaxy hanging in the balance, the Jedi's judgment was clouded by his attachments. You see, the evil Darth Sidious had recognized Anakin's love for Padme, his pregnant wife, as the young Jedi's weakness. And Sidious preyed upon it mercilessly, firmly planting the erroneous yet powerful belief in Skywalker that the Dark Side of the Force was the only path to Padme's salvation. So, as Sidious lay helpless at Jedi Master Mace Windu's feet after Windu had skillfully defeated him, and the Jedi Master was about to extinguish Sidious's life and along with it the evil Sith plot to dominate the galaxy, Anakin came to the Dark Lord's defense, summarily executing his fellow Jedi Windu and tragically joining forces with Sidious, transforming himself at that very moment from "chosen one" Anakin Skywalker to evil incarnate Darth Vader.

Those few moments drastically changed the course of the galaxy and caused thousands of years of despair—and laid the foundation for the three subsequent *Star Wars* installments, which were, of course, the three first installments to be released, as *Star Wars*, *The Empire Strikes Back*, and *Return of the Jedi*. Episodes four, five and six in the saga's chronology, but one, two and three in our own.

Whether you happen to be familiar with George Lucas's opus or not (I have my son's involvement with the series to thank for my warm re-acquaintance with it), Yoda's teachings ring true. For one can only lead objectively if devoid of outside influences. And these influences can range from fear about losing loved ones to investment portfolios to belonging to racial and ethnic groups. It is a sad and unfortunate reality that in most cases we feel we can be represented only by those who look like us, have the same customs or faith, or share our ethnic background. And that, dear reader, is one of the great tragedies of our time.

When will we truly transcend the relatively superficial characteristics that differentiate us? When will those who elect leaders look to the substance of the candidates before them instead of their race, ethnicity or gender? When will those who lead make decisions for the overall good, and not to please one constituency or another? Is a truly objective leader, once who transcends superficiality, electable today? Would he or she be able to lead effectively in a democracy?

Maybe those who run for office should do so anonymously . . . wait a minute, maybe we're onto something here. OK, hear me out:

The candidates are presented as A, B and C. Their positions on all issues of importance to the electorate are put forth in writing, on a single Web site where there are no differences in style or format; only the content is different. There are no speechwriters, strategists or aides. The candidates write their own position documents.

Debates are held in a similar manner. Questions are put forth and answers are returned, all written directly by the candidates. All we know about them is, with a nod to a leader who clearly transcended attachments, the content of their character. There is no fundraising, no lobbying, no special interests. We elect a catalog of ideas, contained within a human being. We cannot allow superficialities to cloud our judgment, because we are not privy to the superficialities.

Pipe dream? Perhaps. *The Dating Game* for a nation? Maybe. All sorts of valid reasons why it would never work? For sure.

The only way that we will truly choose our leaders for the right reasons? Absolutely.

So Much Time

September 30, 2007

GIL GRISSOM AND his CSI team in Las Vegas use all sorts of cool science to allow forensic evidence on and around the dead to cut through the web of lies typically spun by the living. The bad guys don't stand a chance against these geeks (who just happen to look like models—this is TV, after all!). They meticulously gather every last speck of trace evidence from crime scenes, and, back at the lab, throw state-of-the-art equipment, superior intellect, and seemingly endless time at it, invariably discovering what really happened.

I don't doubt that the equipment we see in *CSI: Crime Scene Investigation* really exists. And I'm sure that many of the scientists who make the analysis of forensic evidence their lives' work are as dedicated and intelligent as Grissom and his crew—although I doubt that too many of them look like Jorja Fox and George Eads. What I don't buy, though, is that they are able to spend so much time on each case, unless the actual murder rate in Las Vegas is about one homicide per month.

I'm not really up on the relative workload of crime labs around the country, but I do know that these days almost everything I do is done either in a hurry, under pressure, or at the very least under strict time constraints. The quantity of output seems to be more important than its quality, as long as it meets the bare minimum requirements. If I take any specific task that I do on any given day as an example, I'm typically getting it done in approximately one-third the time that it would take to do it well, and more likely than not, I'm doing it while juggling another task or two. I'm sure I'm not alone here; I think these days we all are getting more done than ever before. But the quality of the work is not what it could be.

A good analogy, perhaps, is cellular telephone service. Today we have our phones with us at all times, and are able to make and receive phone calls from almost anywhere to almost anywhere at reasonable costs. But we also take bad audio quality, frequent failed and dropped calls, and lousy customer service for granted. Back in the day, our landline service was limited to our homes and offices and long distance was prohibitively expensive, but each call was crystal-clear, and there were virtually no dropped or failed calls. The public switched telephone network evolved over decades, and was constantly refined and modernized. No one has spent the time and money necessary to perfect any of the myriad cellular technologies that have existed or that currently exist, not in small part because they are replaced by a better technology long before they could ever have been perfected. Ubiquity and cost rule, and quality is only important in that new technologies must at least meet minimum quality requirements, but it is clear that we are perfectly willing to lower the quality threshold in order to increase ubiquity or lower cost.

When the delectable Sara Sidle (played by the aforementioned Fox) spends hours upon hours scouring a crime scene and collecting trace evidence, or when the dashing Nick Stokes (played by the aforementioned Eads) seemingly takes days to, say, reassemble a severely shattered mirror, there are no distractions, no interruptions. Their cell phones only bring them information that will help them solve the current case, never new problems or unrelated issues. They are able to spend absolutely all of their time on the specific task at hand, and only once it is completed do they go on to the next task. Fascinatingly, there is never another murder that requires their attention while they are still working on the previous homicide. Must be an unwritten rule among Las Vegas criminals.

So when I watch *CSI*, I don't envy the crime lab team's high-tech equipment. My team of Macs is easily up to any task on my list. And as to the fact that CSI Chief Gil Grissom gets to interact with an attractive bunch, well, given my principal business partner (my lovely wife) I have no complaints in that department either. But when I see those guys spend what seems like weeks to determine that the apparently unrecognizable, repulsive mass in the victim's stomach was actually part of a single strand of linguini made by Montebello, a rare brand favored by the suspect, proving that the victim had, in fact, eaten dinner at the suspect's home the night of the murder . . . I do envy them for the apparently unlimited time they get to spend on their tasks. The tantalizing geeks over at the Las Vegas Crime Lab excel at what they do, because they have the time to do it well.

The Voice of God

October 14, 2007

DANIEL FURILLO, 65, takes his nine-year-old grandson, Tony, to Yankee Stadium for the Yankees home opener against the Red Sox on April 17th, 1951. Upon entering the stadium, little Tony hears what will become his first baseball memory, as a deep, distinguished Voice from above intones the words, "Ladies and gentlemen, welcome to Yankee Stadium." During the rest of the afternoon, Tony is deeply mesmerized by the Voice, as it says magical things like, "Number five . . . Joe DiMaggio . . . center field . . . number five." and "Ladies and gentlemen, your attention please. Now pitching for the Yankees . . . number 17. . . Vic Raschi." Years later, a man named Reginald Martinez Jackson (but better known simply as Reggie Jackson) would express, in his inimitable style, what little Tony Furillo thought that spring day in 1951. Little Tony, you see, was sure he had heard the Voice of God.

"God," in this context, is Bob Sheppard, who, as it happens, made his debut as public address announcer for the Yankees on home opening day, 1951. The Yankee lineup card that day sported names like Rizzuto, Berra, and Mize. A rookie named Mantle. And, of course, the aforementioned Joltin' Joe, in his last year as a Yankee. A total of seven Hall of Famers were on the field that spring afternoon (Yankees Rizzuto, Berra, Mize, Mantle, and DiMaggio, and Red Sox Ted Williams and Lou Boudreau), and of the seven, only the 82-year-old Berra remains with us on the planet. Yet, 57 years and an astonishing 4,500-odd games later, Sheppard still handles PA duties at Yankee Stadium, and in doing so continues to define the quintessential baseball public address announcer. Understated and professional, Sheppard's unique style adds elegance and grace to every Yankee home game. Yankee players' appreciation of Sheppard is exemplified by Derek Jeter, current Yankee captain, who recently indicated that, if he had his way, they would make a recording of Sheppard's voice announcing his (Jeter's) name, for any future occasion where Sheppard is unable to do so himself.

On May 7th, 2000, Sheppard's 50th anniversary season with the Yankees, the club dedicated a plaque in his honor to be placed in the stadium's Monument Park. The plaque is engraved, in part, "Bob Sheppard, Public Address Announcer, 'The Voice of Yankee Stadium.' For half a century, he has welcomed generations of fans with his trademark greeting, 'Ladies and Gentlemen, Welcome to Yankee Stadium.' His clear, concise, and correct vocal style has announced the names of hundreds of players—both unfamiliar and legendary—with equal divine severance, making him as synonymous with Yankee Stadium as its copper facade and Monument Park."

During Sheppard's rookie year at the mic in 1951 he announced his first post-season game, Game One of the 1951 World Series on October 4th, where the Yanks faced the then New York Giants, (including another rookie, Willie Mays). Sheppard went on to announce 121 consecutive post-season games, a streak that ended just a few days ago when he was unable to attend 2007 Divisional Series games due to a bronchial infection. Last year, Sheppard missed the Yankee's home opener for the first time since 1951, having thrown out his left hip the night before. It is sad to see these streaks end, yet at the same time their demise serves to bring them to our attention and allow us to consider just how rare and precious they are.

Tony Furillo, now 65, takes his nine-year-old grandson, Daniel, to Yankee Stadium for the Yankees home opener against the Devil Rays on April 2, 2007. Upon entering The Stadium, little Frank hears what will become his first baseball memory, as a deep, distinguished Voice from above intones the words, "Ladies and gentlemen, welcome to Yankee Stadium."

Tony feels goosebumps, as he has every time he has heard that particular voice say those particular words.

Voice of God, indeed.

Note: The Furillos are fictional. Everyone (and everything) else is real.

The Ethanol Myth

November 25, 2007

WATCHING *THREE'S COMPANY* (the '70s sitcom starring the late John Ritter, Suzanne Somers, and Joyce DeWitt) was always brutal torture for me. Each episode, as you may remember, was based on some sort of misunderstanding. And while many people enjoy watching others make fools out of themselves by proceeding under the wrong assumptions, I am not amused, but frustrated instead. Watching fictional characters make fictional bad decisions because they rely on the wrong information is difficult enough. But watching real people make bad decisions, often far-reaching bad decisions, due to misunderstandings or misinterpretations, is about as enjoyable to witness as a team of fingernails scraping their way down a dry chalkboard.

The production and use of ethanol as an alternative to gasoline is widely perceived to be the answer to our nation's energy problems. And why not? After all, U.S.-produced ethanol comes from corn, which is abundant and inexpensive here. Gasoline is, of course, refined from petroleum, a scarce, expensive resource we depend on other, mostly hostile, nations to provide for us. So, conventional wisdom goes, ethanol can help reduce our dependence on imported oil. "Everything about ethanol is good, good, good," says Iowa Republican Senator Charles Grassley.

So, what's the misunderstanding?

Sorry, Charlie, but to begin with, corn is probably the worst ethanol source available! Ethanol produced from sugar cane has an energy balance of 8-to-1 (sugar cane ethanol generates eight times more energy than is used to produce, transport, and refine it). Gasoline itself has an energy balance of 5-to-1. But corn's energy balance is only 1.3-to-1, meaning that corn-based ethanol produces barely more energy than is consumed to make it! Some studies have even concluded that making corn-based ethanol actually consumes more energy than the fuel produced. Nevertheless, 20 percent of the U.S. corn crop this year will go toward ethanol production, causing hefty price increases for the corn that is left for other uses. The price of Mexican dietary staple cornmeal tortillas, for example, has risen 60 percent in the last year alone, while corn prices in the U.S. have risen 58 percent, causing higher prices for all sorts of related items like steak (steer are fed on corn) and soft drinks (sweetened with corn syrup).

So, why do we use corn-based ethanol? Politics, that's why! Corn-producing states wield great power in Washington, and thus Congress has lavished more than $50 billion in subsidies and tax credits for ethanol since 1995, of which $10 billion has gone to agribusiness giant Archer Daniels Midland. Oh, and, by the way, Archer has spread over $3 billion in campaign contributions since 2000. Iowa, the largest corn-producing state, happens to hold the first major contest of the presidential campaign season, so presidential hopefuls fall all over themselves lavishing praise on ethanol. Democratic candidate Barack Obama recently reminded Iowans that he wants to raise U.S. production of ethanol to 60 billion gallons by 2030, and rival John Edwards predictably responded by calling for 65 billion gallons by 2025.

But wait. There's more. Contradicting the widely accepted view that ethanol is environmentally friendly, a recent study by

Stanford University atmospheric scientist Mark Jacobson concluded that "ethanol poses an equal or greater risk to public health than gasoline" because the burning of ethanol produces more lung-damaging ozone than the burning of gasoline. In addition, corn growers rely on nitrogen-based fertilizers; rain washes the nitrogen into streams and rivers where it displaces the oxygen in the water, killing marine life.

And more. Ethanol cannot be shipped via existing gasoline pipelines because it readily absorbs water and other impurities. So, ironically, it must be transported by fuel-burning trucks! "We're importing oil from Saudi Arabia and other places to make ethanol," says Cornell University environmental scientist David Pimentel. In order to handle ethanol, existing gas pumps must be retrofitted at a cost of $100,000 per station. And most cars simply can't burn fuel mixtures containing more than 10 percent ethanol because higher concentrations corrode engine parts.

The bottom line? Let's say that Barbara Eden, in all her scantily-clad 1967 glory, would appear before us today, slap palms on elbows and give her signature magical blink, and suddenly all of our gas stations would be retrofitted to dispense ethanol, all of our cars would be able to burn 100 percent ethanol fuel, and our existing gasoline pipelines would suddenly be able to transport ethanol. We would then be able to consume every drop of ethanol produced in the U.S, which would replace 1.5 million barrels of oil per day, which is—hold on to your hats—7 percent of America's daily oil consumption. No typo. Seven.

Plant-based energy sources may well prove to be important to America's future. But as long as our legislators focus on corn as the chief source of ethanol, we are simply headed down the wrong path. As plant scientist Roger Samson puts it, "If this is a horse race, the U.S. has bet on a donkey."

Note: This essay is based on a briefing that appeared in the October 5, 2007 issue of The Week.

Ron Wants Out

December 2, 2007

RON WANTED OUT. Sure, he had been given 10 percent of the company, so none of his own money was riding on the deal, but it was structured as a partnership! And his partners, the Nerd and the Whirlwind (as Ron had begun to think of them) had no money, so if the company failed to meet its obligations (which seemed quite likely, thought Ron), creditors could come after him! Personally! Take his car, his home! The few dollars he had hidden under his mattress! I have everything to lose, thought Ron. And now there was talk about going further into debt to increase production.

No. The risk was too high. Ron wanted out. Now.

So on April 12th, less than two weeks after the partnership was officially founded, Ron sold his 10 percent stake in the company to his partners for $800.

Please cup your chin, dear reader, for your jaw is about to drop.

The year was 1976. Ron's last name was (and still is, of course) Wayne. Ron's partners were Steve Wozniak (the "Nerd") and Steve Jobs (the "Whirlwind"). The partnership was Apple

Computer. Ron Wayne's 10 percent stake in Apple, which he sold for $800 in 1976, would have been worth $244 million in 1991, over $500 million in 2000, and a staggering $2.5 billion today, based on Apple's closing price of $182.22 per share last Friday November 30th. Bummer.

So, did Ronald Gerald Wayne become bitter and forlorn? Has he spent the rest of his life regretting his 1976 decision? Quite the contrary. Twenty years later Wayne stated, "I have never had the slightest pangs of regret, because I made the best decision with the information available to me at the time. My contribution was not so great that I felt I had been diddled with in any way." As Owen W. Linzmayer puts it in his book *Apple Confidential*, "A person of lesser character might be paralyzed with bitterness and self-doubt after walking away from such fame and fortune, but not Ron Wayne. He put it behind him and got on with his life." Admirable chap, Mr. Wayne. Admirable indeed.

We all make scores of decisions every day. We subconsciously classify them as major, minor, and somewhere in between based on their impact on our lives, or, more accurately, what we perceive to be their impact on our lives. Our perception is often misguided, sometimes spectacularly so. Say, for example, you decide to take a different route home, perhaps because of traffic concerns. A minor decision, of course. Not so minor, however, if you die in a car accident on the way. Or, to use a more positive example, not so minor if you got home safely but would have been in an accident on the way home had you used your customary route. In the latter case you would never know how major your decision was. In the blithe ignorance of your mind, you just went home using an alternate route, and that was that.

Sometimes the decisions are major, but not for the reasons we think they are. We evaluate job opportunities based on things like compensation and potential for future growth. But just a few months into a new job, let's say, you meet the person with whom you'd like to spend the rest of your life. Or, your perfect soulmate happened to work at the job you rejected because it paid $10K less per year, so the two of you never meet.

Every decision, minor as it may appear, has the potential to dramatically impact our lives. And the criteria we use to make major decisions are seldom as significant to our lives as other, unforeseen consequences of those decisions. Because, frustratingly, we simply have very little information on which to base most of the decisions we make, so our criteria consist of conjecture more than reality; extrapolation more than fact.

I've hired people based on a half-hour personal interview and little else. I've also hired people aided by executive search consulting firms, where the candidate was exhaustively interviewed and tested and found to be perfectly matched for the opportunity at hand. I have found there to be absolutely no relationship between the time and effort expended to determine an individual's qualification for a job, and her actual performance. If anything, the relationship has been inverse. Why? Simple. Not enough information. It seems that there are so many variables involved that to attempt to cover them all amounts to spending your allotted time lost among the myriad trees while never really perceiving the forest.

Circling back to the praiseworthy Ronald Gerald Wayne, the world assumes he made a colossally bad decision back in the spring of '76. Yet he feels no regret. And we must allow for the possibility that his decision was, in the long run, a good one. No question, Wayne would have been materially wealthier had he held on to his Apple stock. But, would his life have been necessarily better? Would he have been happier?

In the end, all we are certain of is that we constantly make decisions without nearly enough information, we base those decisions on criteria which most of the time turns out to be less relevant than other factors, and we never really find out if we made the right decision.

We might as well skip the analysis… and flip a coin!

Life in the Cloud

January 22, 2008

LIFE IN THE Cloud. I thought it was imminent in 2001. At that time I decided to entrust our company's accounting records to a fledgling outfit then known as NetLedger (today a behemoth known as NetSuite). NetLedger was (and NetSuite still is) a Web-based application, or an application that runs on a distant server and users access over the Internet. Heresy in most people's minds at the time, and philosophically adverse to the conventional model: your software and your data (particularly your sensitive accounting data) live on your own computer, or on a server on your own network, under your control. Not on someone else's server. Not on someone else's network.

NetLedger was basically QuickBooks on the Web, exactly what we needed, and it presented a new paradigm. You use your browser to log in and access your data. All you need is an Internet connection. You can be in your office, or in another city, or in another continent. You can be using a Windows PC, a Mac, or a Linux machine. No matter. Your data is in the Cloud.

In 2001 I was certain that NetLedger was a harbinger of a rapidly forthcoming epic shift from local data to remote data; from platform dependence to platform independence; from access based on location to geographical irrelevance. There will soon be, I thought at the time, computers everywhere, and instead of carrying a laptop with us at all times we will simply use the computer that is there (wherever "there" happens to be) to access our data. We will simply log in, and everything will just be there.

It didn't exactly happen that way.

Or, if you take a broader view, it happened exactly that way, but much, much slower than I expected. It is still happening today, and will probably continue to happen for years—until my idealistic world of ubiquitous access to data is complete, probably for my grandchildren to enjoy. Today's kids, however, will not need to migrate to this new world order; they're largely already there. Their mail is on Gmail, accessible on the Web. Their photos are on Flickr. Their lives, down to every intimate detail, are on Facebook. They text and they Twitter. All is Web-based. They use their laptops, their cell phones, their Pearls, their Sidekicks, their iPhones. The platform is irrelevant. Their data is literally spread all over the planet. They live in the Cloud.

Maybe, as productivity guru and all-around cool guy Merlin Mann speculates, Apple's .Mac service will evolve into a repository for all of our data. Maybe Google's Web-based applications will finally make Microsoft Office irrelevant. Maybe we will all have personal servers that house our data, and devices to access it in different ways depending on context.

Or maybe, as is rapidly becoming the case for me today, a combination of the above will propel us to the nirvana of a Cloud-based existence. Whichever way it happens, it *will* happen.

Unless, of course, it doesn't.

The Obama Dilemma

March 16, 2008

PRESIDENT BARRACK OBAMA. The possibility titillates. As our nation, indeed the world, desperately yearns for leadership, here comes a U.S. president with a richly diverse background, endowed with a keen intellect, superb oratorical skills, and exquisite charisma. Obama's election could easily inspire uplifting change, and result in dramatic disruption of tired paradigms. An intelligent, articulate leader with the rare ability to actually bring people together presents a formidable foe for all that ails us, as well as a catalyst for the kind of grass-roots activism not seen in this country for 40 years. True leadership brings with it a can-do attitude, which has been missing in action in this country for far too long.

And wait, there's more. As an added bonus, an Obama presidency would deal racism and bigotry an unprecedented blow, perhaps knocking those two scourges of mankind down, if not out. For racism feeds on ignorance, and bigotry is perpetuated by unsubstantiated words. And unfounded words disintegrate into nothingness when confronted by evidence to the contrary. The unmitigated absurdity of racism would become glaringly evident all over the planet as the United States proudly puts forth a truly great leader that the world can adopt as its own. A beloved statesman whose portrait, like JFK's, will hang in living rooms the world over. A leader who just happens to be black. Simply magnificent. Titillating indeed.

OK, reality check.

Although Obama is most widely criticized for his lack of experience, his intelligence may easily compensate for it, since he is a fast learner and certainly smart enough to realize that it will behoove him to surround himself with people replete with the experience he lacks. No, Obama's relative inexperience is not a concern to me. However, his apparent naïveté with regard to foreign policy, and his liberal views on economic matters, are disturbing.

Senator Obama seems to honestly believe that reasonable dialogue is the only tool required to resolve conflicts. I believe that there are many situations where dialogue clearly does not work and a hard line, albeit perhaps unsavory, is the only way to obtain the desired result. Examples abound—the Middle East, the former Soviet Union, Colombia's fight against the FARC terrorists, and so on ad infinitum. However, it is not the point of this essay to debate the issues. The point is that I do not agree with Senator Obama's apparent reliance on dialogue alone to resolve conflicts.

I also take a much more conservative position than the senator when it comes to economic issues. I am disappointed when I hear Obama speak out against NAFTA, for example, or when I listen to his plans to deal with the mortgage crisis. Again, I will resist the urge to discuss each of those issues; suffice it to say that I am generally a proponent of small government, free trade, and economic laissez-faire, while Obama clearly seems to take opposite positions.

All that said, however, does my disagreement with Obama on a wide range of issues justify my vote for John McCain, his likely opponent in the general election (assuming, of course, that Obama is able to defeat Senator Hillary Rodham Clinton for the Democratic nomination)? Or are my disagreements with Obama petty and insignificant when compared to all the good that can come of an Obama presidency? Are my concerns about economics and foreign policy enough to stop me from voting for a man whose leadership could conceivably bring unprecedented, groundbreaking change?

I've always been a sucker for the bold move, intoxicated by the possibilities of a true sea change. For that reason, I find myself gravitating toward Obama despite my being at odds with many of his fundamental beliefs. For although I know that as president he will make many decisions with which I will disagree, I also know that a mesmerizing leader like Obama can make great things happen.

And who am I to stand in the way of great things?

www.ingramcontent.com/pod-product-compliance
Lightning Source LLC
Chambersburg PA
CBHW030138170426
43199CB00008B/113